GHOSTS

GHOSTS

THE COMPLETE GUIDE TO THE SUPERNATURAL

ZACHARY GRAVES

canary
press

CONTENTS

INTRODUCTION

A belief in ghosts goes back thousands of years and is a feature of many cultures across the world, whether in folk traditions, religious rituals or spiritual beliefs. Today, it continues to be as prevalent as ever. Ghost hunting tours have become very popular, with groups gathering to explore haunted locations. Numerous websites advertise an array of gadgetry to monitor paranormal activity, such as filming and recording phenomena to measure electro-magnetic fields and log changes in temperature. Advice is also offered on how to analyze findings from photos, recordings and logbooks, after the events have taken place.

GHOSTBUSTERS

The huge interest in ghosts is exemplified by the sheer volume of reality television shows based around the supernatural. Investigative programmes are immensely popular, where ghost hunters are filmed in a variety of locations either simply tracking down ghosts and monitoring their activity or actively trying to exorcize them, using a variety of means from persuasion to displays of aggression. These reality TV shows in turn have taken their cue from such landmark films as *The Exorcist* and *Ghostbusters*. Several of the paranormal investigation programmes currently airing on TV purport to be scientifically based, while others function more as entertainment than rigorous scientific enquiry. But whatever their approach, it remains clear from their continuing popularity that the subject of ghosts and paranormal activity continues to fascinate people today, in the 21st century, just as it did our ancestors thousands of years ago.

The Restless Ghost

The belief in ghosts stems from a basic, and very human, fear of death and the unknown, and can be traced back to many ancient religions and folk traditions. In all these different cultures it is commonly believed that when we die our souls live on, not in bodily form, but as 'spirits', 'essences', 'phantoms', 'ghosts' or other disembodied beings. This idea appears to be central to most human civilizations, although there are many different conceptions as to how ghosts live and behave. In some cultures, they appear to return from the afterlife as revenants, sometimes looking exactly as they did in life, to visit friends and family. While in other stories, the ghosts never leave the land of the living, but remain present in the household or workplace where they once resided, watching over the activities of those that they left behind.

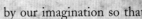

CEASELESSLY WANDERING

Yet despite all the variations in the stories of how ghosts come into being and what they do once they begin to live on as spirits, we find many similarities across different cultures. It is widely believed that a 'wandering' ghost, one who travels ceaselessly and cannot find rest, is the spirit of a person who has been wronged in some way in his or her lifetime. Such people include those who may not have been buried with the proper rites, or may have been badly treated by their family, lovers or friends. As well as this, it is believed that people who have met with terrible accidents, or who have been murdered, may be forced to wander the earth looking for redress. In terms of human psychology, the ghost of a person may function as a reminder of the wrong committed, and can cause a great deal of guilt to be felt on the part of the living. The ghost may be seen as an embodiment of a human feeling of regret, guilt or sense of loss, conjured up by our imagination so that we can continue the relationship with the deceased.

CRIMES OF THE PAST

People who have been victims of crime or mistreatment are often believed to become restless spirits after death; as are those who committed crimes against others. In the past, murderers, thieves and other miscreants were thought to become wandering ghosts when they died, condemned to an afterlife of constant loneliness and misery. Those who were judged to have lived an immoral life, such as prostitutes, might also be thought of as failing to find rest after death. Such ghosts were often conceived of as revenants who had become jealous of the living and who would do everything in their power to do them harm. For this reason, ghosts in many cultures were greatly feared, and thought of as highly dangerous to the living, because of their supernatural evil powers.

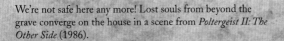

We're not safe here any more! Lost souls from beyond the grave converge on the house in a scene from *Poltergeist II: The Other Side* (1986).

Good or Evil?

This leads us to the question of whether ghosts are seen as malevolent, evil beings who seek to wreak vengeance on the living, or whether we think of them as benevolent spirits of loved ones who remain with us for company, guidance and – strange as it may seem – companionship. Both types of ghosts are widely believed in, although the malevolent kind, by their nature, gain a great deal more attention. In particular, the idea that a ghost can, in some cases, inhabit a living human being, possessing them and making them commit dreadful crimes, is a common and very disturbing theme. In this book, we will be looking at both types of ghost – the good and the bad – and also at cases in which people were believed to be possessed, often causing the victim terrible pain, suffering and even death.

Demonic Possession and Exorcism

We know from history, particularly in medieval times, that societies often attributed instances of severe mental illness in an individual to demonic possession. Such a belief might be a superstition from the folklore of a certain region, but it is also a common thread in major worldwide religions such as Christianity, especially within the Catholic church.

However, some denominations within the Christian church have also condemned this belief and see the fascination with ghosts and the paranormal as unhealthy and immoral. 'Necromancy' or 'bone conjuring' – the attempt to raise the dead through incantations and spells – has been roundly condemned as sinful by various church administrations at different times in history, and

THE WATERTOWN GHOSTS. The ghostly faces of two dead sailors peer out from the bow of their ship, the *SS Watertown*. The sailors were a pair of ex-shipmates named Courtenay and Meehan who had been buried at sea and continued to haunt their old vessel whenever it ventured into the Pacific Ocean. This picture was taken in 1925.

continues to be looked on with suspicion in many quarters, especially among those of a religious persuasion.

TRUE CASES

Today the belief in demonic possession persists and is a stock motif of much horror fiction, whether in books, films or on TV. It takes on a more sinister aspect, though, when we come to real instances in which individuals – often children or young people – have been believed to be possessed by a devil. In this book, we will take a look at some of these cases, such as the story of Robbie Mannheim (not his real name), on whom the film *The Exorcist* was based, as well as that of Anneliese Michel, a young German woman from a devout Catholic family. In Robbie Mannheim's case, the exorcisms appeared to do him no harm, and he went on to lead a normal life; in Anneliese Michel's, she was subjected to so many rites of purgation and exorcism that she eventually died of starvation and exhaustion. After a long delay, Michel's parents and the two priests that performed the exorcisms were taken to court and charged with neglectful homicide. The sad case of Anneliese Michel demonstrates that what may appear to be harmless superstition or fervently held religious belief, can in fact result in horrific tragedy.

THE SÉANCE AND THE OUIJA BOARD

While the reality of these cases, in which the belief in demonic possession is taken to an extreme, may be appalling, they are most unusual in modern times. For most of us, the belief in ghosts and the paranormal is nothing to do with demonic possession, but is more akin to the thrill we get from a horror film, or the pleasantly scary sensation of entering an old building reputed to be haunted.

However, there are those who wish to investigate further, among them the mediums and psychics who believe themselves able to contact the dead and who conduct séances using ouija boards and other devices, whether in private, for friends and family or as a form of public entertainment.

SPIRITUALISM

This idea of conversing with the dead has its roots in very ancient practices, across many cultures, but today it is still prevalent. In the West, it became especially popular in the late 19th and early 20th century, when spiritualism arose.

There were many kinds of spiritualist movements, including what was known as 'Spiritism', which was based on five books written by Allan Kardec, whose real name was Hypolite Rivail. In these books, he wrote about a series of phenomena that he thought were evidence of disembodied intelligence, or spirits. Kardec had many followers, including the author of the *Sherlock Holmes* series, Arthur Conan Doyle.

Even today the movement continues to be a force in many parts of the world, especially in Latin America, where it is known as 'Espiritismo'. Adherents believe that spirits affect our health, our luck and other aspects of our lives, and that they can be contacted through 'espiritistas' or mediums. The mediums attempt to contact the dead in 'misas', which are rather like séances, but also contains elements of magic and ritual.

INVESTIGATING THE PARANORMAL

The idea of contacting the dead and possibly encountering benevolent ghosts who have something to tell us, either about their past lives or our own future, fascinates the public today, not just in the West, but all over the world. Paranormal phenomena such as ghostly presences, unexplain-

able sounds of knocking or footsteps, pinpoints of light, 'cold spots', shadows or unusual currents of air or wind, are constantly being probed and challenged, both from a scientific and intellectual point of view. This is partly because the technology for measuring such phenomena has vastly improved, so that sounds, images, changes in air temperature and alterations in electro-magnetic fields thought to be caused by the presence of ghosts are now all subject to careful calibration and analysis. Yet the accuracy of these findings continues to be a constant source of controversy, often from scientists who believe that such attempts to measure paranormal phenomena are inherently flawed. Despite these misgivings, there continue to be scientists who are open to the concept of the paranormal realm, and view it as a suitable subject for continuing scientific investigation.

Festivals and Celebrations

It has been argued by anthropologists that in Western culture not enough attention is paid, on an emotional or practical level, to the death of a loved one. Mourning may take place in a hurried way and after the funeral there may be no further acknowledgement of the death, at least in public. In other cultures, as many commentators have pointed out, this is not the case. Ancestors are revered and the deaths of family members remembered in elaborate annual rituals and ceremonies, which often include an element of entertainment as well as grief and mourning.

HONOURING THE DEAD

Examples of such ceremonies include the Hungry Ghost Festival that takes place among Taoist and Buddhist followers in many countries, particularly in the East. A ritual that takes place in Mexico is the Day of the Dead, which honours deceased family members in festivities that sometimes last all day and night, and include holding picnics and vigils at the graveside of lost loved ones. In comparison, the European and American festival of Halloween seems much more oriented towards folklore, with an emphasis on enjoyable, non-religious traditions aimed mainly at entertaining children with games such as apple bobbing, carving jack'o'lanterns from pumpkins and 'trick or treating'.

Magic and Ghosts

The festival of Halloween draws much of its appeal from remnants of occult traditions such as sorcery and witchcraft, rather than from religious rites and rituals. This is partly because the connection between magic and raising the dead, known as necromancy, was frowned upon by the Christian church as sinful and evil during the medieval period. Such an attitude still prevails today in some quarters, whether among religious folk, non-believers or scientists, yet this does not prevent many people from continuing to try to contact dead relatives in the hope that communion with the dead will help them to solve pressing problems in their own lives, or assuage their guilt about how they treated loved ones in life.

THE UNDERWORLD

In fact, the belief in magic as a way of controlling events in the afterlife goes back centuries, to the Egyptian *Book of the Dead*, a funerary text used up until about 50 BC. This text includes a number of magic spells that could be used to help a recently deceased person travel through the underworld, called the 'duat'. The book was written in hiero-glyphic script on a papyrus scroll, often illustrated with pictures of the dead person and the story of their travels into the afterlife, and placed in the burial chamber with the body. The spells might also be written up on the chamber walls, so that the living could keep track of the journey that the deceased made after burial.

Phantoms of the Imagination

For most of us, the realm of the paranormal is a fascinating subject, rather than one that we wish to investigate in any intensive way. We may prefer to learn about it through ghost stories, novels, films and TV shows, rather than setting out on a hunt to discover the truth for ourselves. That may be because we are sceptical, or perhaps because even the most rational among us may be a little wary of delving too far into the occult. Whatever the reason, today there is continuing focus on what one might call 'phantoms of the imagination' – that is, images and tales of ghosts that we find in all areas of popular media.

As well as the numerous 'ghost hunting' reality TV shows, there have been some extraordinary successes in this area in the world of publishing. Among them are the fictional works of authors such as Stephen King and J. K. Rowling, who both deal in the world of the supernatural, albeit from different angles. King included a ghost in his novel *Bag of Bones*, published in 1998, which tells of the ghost of a blues singer haunting the house of a troubled writer, while J. K. Rowling gives ghosts an important part to play in her *Harry Potter* series. Unlike most ghosts, her phantoms are friendly advisers who appear as silvery, translucent entities rather than frightening ghouls. They are usually the dead souls of wizards, rather than those of ordinary people. Among her cast of generally amicable ghosts are Moaning Myrtle, Nearly Headless Nick, The Bloody Baron, Professor Bins, The Grey Lady and The Fat Friar.

In much modern literature, the ghosts described are not literal phantoms but are more likely to be psychological entities, so that the reader is never sure whether the characters in the novel have actually seen a ghost, or whether they are simply suffering from psychotic delusions. This play between the real and the imaginary, between sanity and madness, between the corporeal and the disembodied, has proved to be a very fruitful subject for literature and art since the days of the Romantics in the 18th century. It continues to lie at the heart of many ghost tales in modern fiction, whether in short stories, novels, films or on TV.

Ghosts on Screen

In recent years, many ghost stories and novels have also been adapted for the screen. The story by Washington Irving, first published in 1820 as *The Legend of Sleepy Hollow*, concerns a headless horseman who commits a series of murders. In 1999, it was released on film with the shortened title of *Sleepy Hollow*.

In conclusion, it seems that our fascination with the paranormal realm, including ghosts and other phenomena, looks set to continue into the future. Whether or not we actually believe in the existence of ghosts, many of us are curious to know more about the world of the supernatural, and especially what happens to us after we die… before we finally find out the truth for ourselves.

Section One

PHANTOMS OF THE PAST

EARLY ORIGINS

The word 'ghost' is derived from the Old English 'gast', which is related to the German word 'geist', connected to the English words 'mind', and 'spirit'. It is also related to the Old Norse word 'geisa', which means to rage. These words reflect the idea of the ghost, from earliest times, being close to that of the spirit, with an added feature that the spirit may be restless or in a state of fury.

The Wild Hunt

One of the most thrilling examples of ghosts as figures of fury is in the ancient European myth of the Wild Hunt. In this story, a phantom group of huntsmen on horseback, with a pack of baying hounds, thunder across the sky in search of prey. The huntsmen are the ghosts of great leaders, kings and legendary figures of the past. Seeing them career across the sky is thought to be a presentiment of disaster such as war, disease or famine, or perhaps a harbinger of death for the person who is unlucky enough to witness it. For this reason, mortals who catch a glimpse of the Wild Hunt are advised to avert their eyes – otherwise, they may find themselves caught up in the chaos and taken to the land of the dead against their will.

The Wild Hunt has been known in different parts of Europe by a variety of imaginative names, including the following: Woden's Hunt, Herod's Hunt, Cain's Hunt, the Ghost Riders, Gabriel's Hounds, The Ride of Asgard and The Devil's Dandy Dogs.

THE BREATH OF LIFE

The Old English word 'gast' was also used as an alternative to the Latin 'spiritus', meaning 'breath'. In ancient times, many believed that the real essence of any living thing, be it animal or human, resided in the breath and that the spirit might live on in the last exhalation of breath by a dying person. This 'spirit' or 'breath' could be good or evil. It could inhabit the living, entering a person's body so that they were possessed. In most beliefs of this kind, the possession was thought to be evil.

It is not until the 14th century that our modern meaning of the word 'ghost' comes into being. In Middle English, the form of English spoken during the medieval period, we find the first references to our modern concept of the ghost – that is, the idea of the soul of a dead person, who may appear to the living in visible form. However, from his time, the word 'ghost' continues to be used in quite a general way, to mean soul, spirit, shadow, after-image, an unearthly presence and so on.

Phantom Magyar Horsemen thunder across the night sky in the Hungarian version of *The Wild Hunt*.

SPOOKS, WRAITHS AND SPECTRES

At the same time as the word 'ghost' began to be commonly used, a number of other evocative terms also came into being. In America, the word 'spook' was borrowed from Dutch, while in Scotland, 'wraith' was used to describe all manner of supernatural apparitions. 'Wraith' comes from a Scottish dialect, and was taken up by the fantasy writer J. R. R. Tolkein, who used it to describe the creatures known as the Ringwraiths in his alternative world. Like the phantoms of the Wild Hunt, the Ringwraiths were ghostly riders. Also known as the Black Riders, Dark Riders or Nine Riders, Tolkein describes them as nine horsemen who are loyal servants of the evil Sauron, and who are much feared for their merciless acts of brutality committed in his name.

Other words for ghosts, with slight variations, include 'phantom', derived from the Greek 'phantasma', 'spectre' from the Latin 'spectrum' and 'shade' from the Latin 'umbra', which references the idea of a supernatural being from the dark underworld. Less common words for 'ghost' include 'haint', used widely in the American South, and 'bogie', an Ulster Scots term.

THE POLTERGEIST

In addition to the many words for ghost, there are various types of ghosts themselves. One of these is the poltergeist, whose name comes from a German word literally meaning 'singing' (or 'noisy') ghost. The poltergeist is traditionally thought of as a troublesome ghost who haunts a house, moves objects around and makes banging noises in the night.

The poltergeist may be feared as a demon, threatening and destructive, or may simply be seen as an irritating nuisance. Some people believe that poltergeists may be former residents of the house, who are jealous of the incomers, and wish to drive them out. Other people suggest that the poltergeists may be the restless spirits of people who were wronged in life, or who may have experienced trauma in the house where they still reside. In some cases, even today, people will have their houses exorcised by a priest to rid themselves of a poltergeist, believing that this process will banish the restless spirit for ever. Instances of poltergeists have been reported in many parts of the world, and seem to be a part of the folkloric beliefs of most cultures. In many cases, poltergeists are thought to be connected with the presence of teenagers in a house. The theory is, that the poltergeists tap into the turbulent emotions experienced by many teenagers, causing inanimate objects to move around of their own accord.

'THE STONE-THROWING DEVIL'

One of the first reports of poltergeists comes from the late 17th century, when a pamphlet was published on 'Lithobolia', or 'the Stone-Throwing Devil', by a man named Richard Chamberlain, a government official in New England, USA. In 1682, Chamberlain boarded at a tavern run by George and Alice Walton and recorded the damage wreaked by the poltergeists that apparently haunted the house. His introduction to the pamphlet read as follows:

'...Being an Exact and True account (by way of Journal) of the various actions of infernal Spirits or (Devils Incarnate), Witches or both: and the great Disturbance and Amazement they gave to George Waltons family at a place called Great Island in the county of New Hampshire in New England, chiefly in throwing about (by an Invisible hand) Stones, Bricks, and Brick-Bats of all sizes, with several other things, as Hammers, Mauls, Iron-Crows, Spits, and other

Utensils, as came into their Hellish minds, and this for space of a quarter of a year.'

Stories of poltergeists were reported throughout the centuries that followed, and today continue to be one of the most commonly witnessed forms of ghost contact.

THE 'FETCH'

Another type of ghost is the 'fetch'. This is the disembodied spirit of a living person.

The 'fetch' most commonly appears to a friend or relative at the exact moment that the living person is about to die. This idea of the 'fetch' helps to explain the commonly reported phenomenon when a person dies, a friend or relative will report having a strong memory of them, or desire to contact them again, only to find that at the exact moment they had this impulse that person had passed away. 'Fetch light' or 'fetch candle' is a term used to describe a light that appears at night and supposedly foretells the death of the person who sees it.

THE REVENANT

Another type of ghost is the revenant, an animated corpse who returns from the grave to visit the living. In most cases, the purpose of the reve-

The Ghostly Drummer of Tedworth. An early representation of poltergeist activity. After the frontispiece to Glanville's *'Saducissmus Triumphatus'* of 1683.

nant is to terrorize or wreak revenge on the living, out of anger, jealousy or spite. In some cases, revenants may return from the grave to see their loved ones again and provide comfort and reassurance to those grieving for them. The term comes from the French 'revenir', to come back.

At the basis of stories of the revenant is a primal fear that the dead will come back to destroy the living. This comes, in most instances, from a feeling of guilt – either because of maltreatment of the dead person in life, or from a more generalized sense that the dead do not deserve to die, any more than the living deserve to live. In such instances, there is a troubling perception that death comes randomly, often to those who least deserve it, while others survive quite happily for no reason other than luck.

VAMPIRES, WEREWOLVES, AND ZOMBIES

In medieval Europe, the fear of revenants seeking revenge on the living took a terrifying form – the widespread belief in the vampire. The attributes of the vampire, as a reanimated corpse, included such features as bleeding orifices, long fingernails, pale skin and pointed teeth. There was also a detailed mythology as to how the vampire would stalk and bite its victims, thus claiming them as living corpses. In the same way, and at the same period, a body of belief also rose up about other supernatural, and largely vindictive, creatures such as the shapeshifting werewolf.

In other parts of the world, at different epochs, many variations on the theme arose, including that of the zombie. The notion of the brain-dead, emotionless zombie as a 'walking corpse' originally comes from the West African and Haitian voodoo tradition. In recent years, it has been expanded on by filmmakers and fiction writers, and a notable feature added – that the zombie wants to eat the flesh of the living, thus eventually destroying humankind altogether in an apocalyptic plague.

FORMS OF DECAY

What characterizes all these revenants – the vampire, the werewolf and the zombie – is a preoccupation with the physical, material body. In the case of the vampire and the zombie, there is an emphasis on the peculiar, and horrifying, forms of decay of the body after death, and our very human, yet doomed, attempts to escape our fate. In the myth of the werewolf, too, we see a fascination with bodily change and with mental deterioration – what we would now call mental illness – that accompanies it. All these stories concern bodily death, change and transformation, and how the human spirit survives, or is corrupted, by the process.

THE GHOST AS 'SPIRIT' OR 'BREATH'

In contrast to this, the ghost remains, in most cultures, an insubstantial creature. The ghost is what remains after the body has gone, whether buried, burned or simply left to rot. Unlike the vampire, the zombie or the werewolf, the ghost is not a creature of the flesh, it is the 'breath' that has departed from the body, the essence of the deceased that survives once the body is no more. In this sense, the ghost is quite distinct from vampires, zombies and werewolves – although, of course, as a supernatural member of the undead it may have some features in common with them.

It must also be pointed out here that the word 'ghost' is often used, in a general way, to refer to any supernatural being. However, this should not prevent us from understanding that 'ghost' – as 'spirit', 'breath' or 'essence' – has a specific history and meaning.

THE GHOST MANIFESTED

In most cultures of the world, we find a traditional belief in ghosts as the souls or spirits of the dead, who appear to the living in visible form. This form may take many different shapes: in some cases, tales may be recounted of a 'presence', especially inside a room, which can be felt, but not seen or heard. In other cases, we find reports of dark shapes or shadows flitting about, half seen. Other people give accounts of seeing translucent wisps or vapours that hang trembling in the air and then disappear.

In the case of the ghost known as the poltergeist, its presence is said to be felt by the noises it makes and by its alleged ability to move small objects around the house, sometimes throwing and breaking them. Finally, there are the stories of ghosts who appear as exact replicas of the deceased, although perhaps paler, thinner and more sickly. In the Egyptian *Book of the Dead*, the individuals are thought to appear exactly as they did in life, down to details of their style of dress.

THE WHITE LADY

In general, ghosts are said to appear as solitary individuals, wandering the earth in a lonely, unhappy existence, unable to rest. They may come back to haunt particular places that they frequented in life, often for a purpose – to tell of a crime that was committed there, or to warn of a future disaster. One such solitary ghost is The White Lady, a legend that appears in many different cultures around the world. This ghost is said to be the troubled spirit of a woman wronged by her husband or fiancé in life. She is often dressed in Victorian apparel, and usually wearing a long black veil. Seeing her is a very bad portent and may signify the onlooker's imminent death, or the death of someone close to them.

However, as well as the common solitary ghost, there are also stories of ghosts appearing in dozens or hundreds such as 'phantom armies', ghost ships and ghost trains. Ghost ships, in particular, have been a popular theme in folklore since the 18th century, when many sailors died in shipwrecks at sea. A classic tale is that of the *Flying Dutchman*, a ship that sails the sea with a ghostly crew, forever condemned to remain out of contact with the living and unable to dock at any port. Legends surrounding the history of the *Flying Dutchman*

vary, but some allege that a dreadful crime was committed on board and that the crew have been punished by wandering the seas as ghosts. As with the legend of the White Lady, seeing the ship is thought to presage death or disaster.

THE ARMOURED GHOST

Today, our ideas about how ghosts manifest themselves has been very much influenced by representations of them in art and popular culture. In English Renaissance theatre of the 16th and early 17th century, ghosts were often shown as dressed in armour – perhaps the most famous example of this is the ghost of Hamlet's father, who appears dressed in full battle regalia. However, there were problems with this, since the armoured ghosts tended to make a terrible clanking noise on stage and instead of frightening the audience, often reduced them to fits of laughter.

By the 19th century, the armoured ghost had become a cliché and directors had begun to solve this problem by emphasizing the 'invisibility' of the ghost, draping them in sheets so that they could move about the stage lightly. This was a complete departure from the traditional image of the Renaissance ghost, as well as from 'stage ghosts' of the classical Greek and Roman era.

SPOOKY GHOSTS

For a time, it seemed that audiences were satisfied with the new 'spooky' ghosts flitting about draped in sheets, or diaphanous clothing. However, it was not long before the sheeted ghosts, too, became a figure of fun. This problem, too, was eventually solved using modern lighting effects and make-up techniques, both on stage and on screen. Today, these special effects have become extremely sophisticated, requiring a high degree of skill, so that ghosts are now far more realistic than their predecessors.

'I am thy father's spirit, doomed for a certain term to walk the night'. The Ghost of Hamlet's father demands that Hamlet avenge his murder in Shakespeare's play. According to legend, the Ghost was originally played by Shakespeare himself. *Hamlet, Act I Scene V*.

ANCESTOR WORSHIP

The belief that the dead live on and can revisit the living as ghosts, is a feature of most early cultures across the world. From ancient times human beings have believed that each individual person has a soul or spirit which continues to survive once that person has died. There is also a belief that the souls of those who have died must be ritually worshipped to prevent them becoming restless, angry or jealous of the living.

This fear is allied to animism, a common belief in primitive cultures that inanimate objects, such as trees, and natural phenomena, such as wind and fire, also have spirits or 'essences'. It is believed that these spirits must be respected and appeased if human beings are to live peacefully within the natural world. This fundamental notion, which occurs universally, has been labelled 'animism' and demonstrates an early fear of upsetting the natural order of life – in death, this idea is mirrored. There is a concern that ancestors will come back as revenants to wreak havoc on those still living, because they are angry that they have been banished from life. The afterlife, in this view, is seen as a place where the souls of the dead are condemned to survive in a bleak, dark, underworld where they may be lonely, starving and in pain.

BANISHING THE GHOST

To prevent these unfortunate souls from seeking revenge for their fate, sacrifices must be made and the spirits appeased by being given food and drink. Such rituals have an ancient history stretching back for centuries and still occur to this day, in the Chinese Hungry Ghost Festival or in the Mexican Day of the Dead.

Many religious practices are also designed to keep the dead from coming back and making trouble. Many funeral rites and burial customs, such as binding the corpse, have the specific intention of preventing the dead from escaping the grave. In addition, religious rituals such as exorcism, in which incense and bells are used, have the specific purpose of banishing ghosts, or spirits, from continuing to live on whether in a person or place.

WILLIAM HOPE, ghost photographer (1863-1933). Hope founded the spiritualist society known as the Crewe Circle. His work was popular after World War One, when many bereaved people were desperate to find loved ones beyond the grave. His deception of using multiple exposure techniques to render the ghosts was publicly exposed in 1922.

LEFT: A woman mourns for her husband, a man's ghostly face swoops over the body.

RIGHT: A young woman's ghostly face appears as if floating above the sitters, draped in a cloak.

GHOSTS OF THE PAST

Ghosts appear in some of the earliest civilizations known to man, including that of Mesopotamia, which today includes Iraq, Syria and parts of Turkey and Iran. The ghosts of the ancient Mesopotamian cultures of Sumeria, Babylonia, Akkadia and Assyria, were thought to come into being at the time of an individual's death and would travel to the underworld, where they would form part of a community that, in many ways, was comparable to the world of the living.

As in many traditions, the relatives and friends of those who had died often made offerings of food and drink for the individual to partake of on the journey to the underworld, and might also continue to do so for a long time afterwards. The living feared the dead, in the sense that ghosts were thought to come back and make trouble, bringing bad luck, disease and even death, if they were not properly honoured and remembered by those they had left behind.

Ancient Egypt

In Ancient Egypt, the belief in an afterlife was an extremely important part of the culture, as is known from the Egyptian *Book of the Dead*, a funerary text that contains magic spells to help a deceased person on their journey to the underworld. The ancient Egyptians believed in the concept of *khu*, or the soul, which was represented by an ibis bird. Later, the soul became divided into five parts – the heart, the shadow, the name, the spirit and the soul. After death, the person became *akh*, a concept similar to the Western idea of the ghost. The *akh* was able to return from the dead as a revenant, roaming the world and doing good or evil, depending on how it had been treated in life. In particular, the *akh* could cause sickness, nightmares and intense feelings of guilt. It was thought that the *akh* could be contacted by the living and relatives might send it letters offering reassurance or asking for advice.

MAGIC SPELLS FOR THE UNDERWORLD

As with the Mesopotamians, the afterlife was envisioned as a community similar to that of the living. Rich men were often buried with their slaves so that the slaves could continue to look after them in the underworld. Also in the burial

24

chamber would be large quantities of food and a book of spells for use on the journey to the underworld; this would show the person how to fly, to pass through walls, and to call on the gods for help. The book of spells might also instruct the person how to avoid a 'second death' by keeping on breathing and thus ensuring that their name lived on.

One of the great pharaoh's of Ancient Egypt, Akhenaten, tried to demolish the religious belief system of the civilization, declaring himself and his queen, Nefertiti, as the embodiments of Aten, the sun god. In a fit of megalomania, he demolished many of the old temples and tried to stamp out the worship of the ancient pantheon of gods. After his death the priests revived the old religion, and cursed Akhenaten, condemning him to wander as a ghost forever in the desert. Legend has it that to this day travellers through the desert lands of Egypt may come upon Akhenaten still wandering there.

Ghosts of Antiquity

In classical Greece, ghosts were seen as feeble imitations of the living, with little power over the social world. In Homer's work, they are described as 'a vapour, gibbering and whining into the earth'. Ghosts were thought of as insubstantial, like mist or smoke, but occasionally they might appear in the form they had taken at death, often bearing the wounds that had caused their demise. As time went on, ghosts began to take a more important role in the culture and were imbued with special powers to influence the living, whether for good or evil. Because of this, the Greeks took to holding public ceremonies in which sacrifices were made, and feasts were prepared to honour the dead and avoid their censure. Family ghosts were invited to the feasts and then asked to leave until the follow-

ing year, when the next feasts would take place. One of the first ghosts written about in antiquity appears in the play *Oresteia* by Aeschylus, which was performed in 458 BC, and concerns the ending of a curse on the house of Atreus.

The Romans also believed in ghosts and had a superstition that a ghost would curse a piece of pottery and then place it into a grave, thereby wreaking revenge on an enemy. In Roman literature, there are several accounts of ghosts haunting the living. Plutarch mentions a ghost who frequented the public baths, terrifying the local people with its loud groans and wails. In addition, Pliny the Younger describes a house where a shackled skeleton was buried; only when it was taken out and reburied did the sound of chains being rattled in the house finally cease. We also find some sceptics in Roman literature; Lucian of Samosata recounts the story of the philosopher Democritus, who took up residence in a tomb to prove there were no ghosts in the cemetery at night. Some of the young men where he lived played practical jokes on him, dressing up in black with skull masks, but ever rational, he refused to abandon his experiment.

Ghosts in Medieval Times

The belief in ghosts was widespread in the Middle Ages. Some believed that evil ghosts could be banished by demanding their purpose in the name of Jesus Christ, while the good ones would not be frightened by hearing the Holy Name. Ghosts were generally regarded as dead souls in waiting, on their way to heaven or hell and residing in purgatory for the time being. In accordance with Christian morality, it was believed that dead souls were forced to atone for their sins by experiencing the same sufferings that they had wreaked on

others during their lifetimes; for example, the ghost of a man who had shouted abuse at his servants was condemned to tear off and swallow parts of his own tongue as a punishment for his bad behaviour in the past.

The medieval ghost varied in appearance from being a wispy wraith to taking on more of a substantial form as a solid human being who might have to be restrained or fought with. Ghosts were usually male and generally envisioned as pale shadows of their former selves, dressed in grey rags and looking thoroughly miserable. In some cases, stories were told of ghostly armies who continued night after night to fight the bloody battles that had ended their lives.

THE SIN OF NECROMANCY

Necromancy is an ancient form of magic in which spirits of the dead are summoned. This, it is claimed, can be done by unearthing dead bodies or by the use of magic spells. In medieval times, necromancers often boasted that their art enabled them to foretell the future, or control the will of a living person, sometimes driving them mad as a punishment for wrongdoing. The rituals of necromancy included sorcery using magic circles, wands, bells and incantations. The necromancer might wear the clothing of the deceased or even mutilate and consume parts of the corpse, carrying out these gruesome ceremonies in graveyards and other melancholy, lonely places.

The practice of necromancy is part of the 'black arts' or the occult, and as such was vigorously opposed by the Christian church. It has an ancient history dating back to early civilizations in Babylon, Egypt, Greece and Rome. In Greek mythology, heroes often travel to Hades to claim the dead souls there. Later, 'bone conjuring', or raising the dead, was specifically condemned by the Christian church, although in actual fact some

clerics dabbled in it, combining occult practices with Christian doctrine.

Ghosts in the Bible

The Jewish and Christian religions have an ambiguous attitude to the idea of ghosts. Often the concept is dismissed as irreligious, belonging to folklore, or worse, demonology, rather than to the Judao-Christian faith. In the Hebrew *Torah*, ghosts are not often mentioned and there are strict instructions in the Book of Deuteronomy for the faithful to avoid dabbling in the occult. However, there is a story in the Book of Samuel about King Saul summoning the Witch of Endor to summon the dead spirit of Samuel. It seems that the world of the occult, including ghosts and spirits, was very much feared by the early Jewish leaders and regarded as outside the province of religious belief.

GHOSTS: FRIEND OR FOE?

In the Christian religion, a similar attitude prevailed, although some Christian sects taught that ghosts are beings who are on their journey to heaven and have been sent back by God to teach the living about the need for repentance of their sins. At the same time, Christians were warned not to trouble the spirits, since they might be demons who were lying in wait to deceive people and lead them away from God. Supernatural occurrences, such as seeing orbs of light or transparent bodies moving as if they were ghosts, were often attributed to the works of the Devil. The biblical book of Corinthians claims that 'even Satan disguises himself as an angel of light'.

GHOSTS AROUND THE WORLD

Ghosts of different kinds appear in almost all cultures around the world. It seems that there is a common human belief that souls live on after death and that those who have suffered poor treatment in life may come back to haunt the living. In addition, many cultures hold religious rituals and ceremonies to honour the dead — and, most importantly, to prevent them causing trouble to those who have lived on.

THE FLESH-EATING DEMON OF INDIA

In India, ghosts are known as *bhoots* or *bhuts*. There are many legends as to how they come into being, but in general they are thought of as transmigrating souls who have encountered some difficulty in their journey after death. They may have failed to get into heaven or nirvana, perhaps because their relatives have neglected to conduct the proper burial rites. Alternatively, they may come back to seek redress when they have been wronged, for example, if they have been murdered.

In Hindu mythology, there are certain types of evil spirits that may haunt graveyards. One of these is called *baital*, a type of vampire, while another is *pishacha*, a demon akin to a zombie. The *pishacha*, which feasts on the flesh of the dead, is said to have big, bulging red eyes and engorged veins. It has dark skin and speaks a language known as Paishachi. As with the Western demon, the *pishacha* can take possession of a living person

Indian demon vampires. The baital escaped through the air shocking his captors . Wood engraving 1870.

causing all sorts of problems, from madness to disease. *Pishashas* are discouraged from doing this by the performance of certain chants or mantras, designed to expel the evil spirit (as in exorcism). Offerings of food and drink may also be made as part of religious rituals to appease the *pishacha*.

THE 'HUNGRY GHOST' OF TIBET

Ghosts are a central part of the Tibetan belief system, expressed most commonly in the Buddhist religion practised in the country. It is thought that after a human being dies, he or she travels to the ghost world. According to the Tibetans, ghosts have a small throat and a huge stomach so they are permanently hungry. The way to exterminate them is to stab them with a dagger or to catch them in a 'spirit trap'. When they are caught they must be burned, so that they can be released and reborn. The Hungry Ghost Festival is performed throughout Tibet every year so that this process can take place (see pages 33-4).

THE 'YUREI' OF JAPAN

In Japan, the *yurei* are the equivalent of the Western ghost. The word 'yu' means 'faint', while 'rei' denotes the soul. It is believed that after death the soul leaves the body and waits to be reunited with its ancestors, when it will join them to protect the members of the family that are still alive. However, in some cases, as when an individual suffers a violent death, the soul may become a *yurei* who stays on earth. Only when the correct rituals are performed can the *yurei* leave the physical world and continue on its journey to the afterlife.

The *yurei* is thought to be clothed in white, the colour that was once used for burial kimonos. Its hair will be long and black, and may also be tangled or unkempt. The limbs of the ghost will be limp, and it may altogether lack a proper bodily form. Sometimes, a pair of blue, green or purple

flames will hover nearby, further emphasizing its surreal nature. The *yurei* can be divided into different types of ghost, all of them having suffered trouble in their lifetimes. *Onryo* are ghosts who come back from the afterlife to seek revenge; *Goryo* are ghosts who have died as martyrs; *Ubume* are female ghosts who have died in childbirth and who may revisit their homes to give sweets to their other children; *Zashiki-warashi* are the ghosts of those who have died as children, who often remain mischievous; and *Funayurei* are ghosts of people who have met their end at sea and who may resemble a mermaid or merman, with fish-like scales on their lower bodies.

In Japan, ghosts are thought to haunt specific places, emerging at night when the spirits meet. The best way of exorcizing them is to help them fulfil their purpose – for example, a family may seek revenge on the ghost's murderer in life, or perform the proper burial rites after a loved one's death. As in the West, a priest might be employed to help perform this exorcism using a variety of means including reciting religious texts. In some areas, holy writings are placed on doorways to prevent the *yurei* from entering.

THE CHINESE 'GUI'

Ghosts, or *gui*, play a very important part in Chinese culture because of the central role of ancestor worship among the people there. There are many different types, among them the *gweilo* or ghost man, a word that is also used in a pejorative sense to mean 'foreigner', and the *mogwai* or devil. Distinctions are made between those who have been executed or killed themselves, those who have died far from home and not received a proper burial, those seeking revenge for a wrongdoing, those who have drowned and those who have been greedy in life and are therefore condemned to remain hungry in death. In addition, there are benevolent ghosts, such as the

NIGHT PARADE OF ONE HUNDRED DEMONS. The Shozenji Temple Fushimi Near Kyoto is Haunted by Hiyakki Yako, painted by R. Gordon Smith.

Hiyakki Yako is a Japanese folk belief that every year supernatural beings, will take to the streets during summer nights. Anyone who comes across the procession will die, unless protected by a special Buddhist sutra.

The Onyro's Revenge. A Japanese yurei returns from the afterlife to seek retribution from his misbehaving wife and her new husband.

ghosts of servants who have returned to continue to help the families they left behind.

In Chinese mythology, the slayer of ghosts and demons is called Zhong Kui. He is a fierce fighter with a dark face and a beard. Legend has it that Zhong Kui is the ghost of a man who killed himself after failing to pass exams that would have ensured him a career as a civil servant. There are many stories of ghosts in Chinese history and mythology. One of these is the story of Tu Po, who was once a minister to the king. The king executed him on false charges, whereupon Tu Po's ghost came back to wreak his revenge, shooting him with a bow and arrow.

In China, a special kind of medium, usually a woman, is used to communicate with the spirits of ancestors. The spirits will be consulted to ask what they need in the afterlife, and a ritual held in which paper effigies are burned to fulfil these needs. In return, the spirit will advise the family on various matters, from financial to spiritual.

POLYNESIAN GHOSTS

In Polynesian culture ghosts, or *quaitu*, play an important role. Many Polynesians believe that after a person dies, his or her spirit travels up to the sky or down to the underworld. In some cases, spirits known as *aumakua* are thought to remain on earth. As in other cultures, ghosts are thought to intervene in human affairs, sometimes for good, sometimes for evil. In some regions, Polynesians tattoo their faces with marks indicating the type of ghost cult they belong to – for example, a spiral symbol may mean that a ghost must ascend on a whirlwind to the sky. There are also many legends and stories concerning ghosts, for example that of Pele, the goddess of fire, who restores her dead lover's ghost to life by using her supernatural powers.

Various kinds of mental and physical illness are explained by the presence of ghosts. This again has parallels in Western culture, especially in the medieval period. If a person begins to exhibit strange behaviour, this may be put down to what is called 'ghost sickness' and the person would be treated with special herbal medicines, or through attempting to contact the ghost and asking it to leave the body of the afflicted person.

MALAYSIAN GHOST MYTHS

Malaysian ghost myths have a very ancient history, but today are still the subject of many popular films. It is believed that when a person dies, the soul leaves the body in the form of a small human, or homunculus, which seeks to feed on the souls of others and may pass into another human being, causing madness, disease and bad luck. The ghost is thought to haunt the deceased's grave for seven days before going on its way. Ghosts are also said to come out under a full moon. One way of destroying a ghost is to tempt it with food so that it transforms itself into an animal in order to eat, at which point it can be killed.

Ghosts, known as *hantu*, come in many different forms. Unusually, many of these are female, such as the *pontianak*, the ghost of a woman who has met her death through childbirth and who may haunt a roadside looking for victims. The *pontianak* may appear as an attractive young woman, entice a man away and then turn into an old hag, biting into his skin and drinking his blood like a vampire. The *pontianak* is usually described as having long hair, fangs and fingernails, and wearing a full-length white dress.

In Indonesia, the *kuntilanak* is a bird with a harsh call who preys on young women, especially virgins, sucking their blood. Another type, the *penanggalan*, who appears with a woman's head and a body of entrails, preys on babies. The baby can be protected by placing branches of a thistle around the doors and windows of a house, to catch the entrails of the ghost.

GHOST FESTIVALS

In many cultures, festivals take place to celebrate and honour the dead. These include the Hungry Ghost Festival, the Day of the Dead and Halloween. All of them share a common goal, which is to appease the ghosts or spirits of the deceased, making sure that they are content so that they do not return to cause trouble to the living.

The Hungry Ghost Festival

This festival, which is sometimes simply called the Ghost Festival, is celebrated by Chinese people all over the world. It takes place on the 15th day of the 7th month according to the Chinese calendar, which is based on the phases of the moon. The day is known as Ghost Day, and on that day it is believed that the dead return to visit the living. In fact, throughout the 7th month, ghosts are said to come out from their home in the underworld to travel to see their relatives.

In order to honour them, Taoist and Buddhist followers make special offerings to the ghosts. They prepare food, make papier mâché models of items such as food, jewellery and luxurious clothing. They may also burn incense, joss paper and sheets of printed paper that are sometimes known as 'hell money'. The participants believe that on the 15th day of the month, the doors of heaven and hell are opened so that the spirits can pass through to the realm of the living.

WELCOMING THE DEAD

In order to welcome the ghosts, large banquets are prepared and the table set for the deceased members of the family, with empty chairs where they would have sat. The Ghost Festival is distinct from the Ancestor Festival, known as Qingming, because all deceased people are acknowledged, that is, younger members of the family, not only the former generations. Various rituals are performed, such as making or buying small paper lanterns and boats and letting them float away on water, which is thought to give the ghosts guidance in finding their way home.

The festival goes back to a Buddhist story about a monk who used his powers of clairvoyance to find out what had happened to his parents. His father had gone to the heavenly realm, while his mother had gone to a lower realm. This was because his mother had hoarded the money left by his father when he died. His mother had become a hungry ghost, with a throat that no food could pass through, but a fat belly causing her to be

permanently hungry. By reciting prayers over a dish of food, the monk was able to reincarnate his mother as a dog. The monk then performed other rites, on the advice of the Buddha, so that his mother could finally be reborn as a human being.

ENTERTAINING THE DECEASED

Today, the Ghost Festival is celebrated with live entertainment, the front seats in a theatre often being left empty for the ghosts. The concerts are held at night, to please the ghosts, and are often very loud in the belief that this is what the ghosts enjoy. Rice and other food is often thrown into the air for the ghosts and incense burned outside people's houses. In the streets, altars are built, with incense and offerings of fresh fruit for the spirits. To guide the ghosts back home after the festivities, people put paper lanterns in the shape of a lotus flower on paper boats and set them on water. When the lanterns go out, the people know that the ghosts have safely completed their journey back to the realm of the dead.

In Japan, the Ghost Festival is known as O Bon, or just Bon, and takes place in July each year. To celebrate the occasion, family members from the big cities often travel to their home towns and villages, and while they are staying there, go to the graves of their ancestors to tend them.

The Day of the Dead

In Mexico, the US and Canada, the Day of the Dead, or Día de los Muertos, is celebrated on 2 November, on the same day as the Catholic All Souls Day. The festival dates back to the ancient civilization of the Aztecs, who used it to honour the 'lady of the dead'. The day before the festival, those who have died as babies and children are remembered, and this is called 'Day of the Little Angels' or 'Day of the Innocents'.

The celebrations include eating, drinking and socializing. Families will also go to graveyards to spend time with their deceased loved ones, building altars there and offering up food and

Trick or Treat ! Evil red-eyed pumpkin heads and ghostly phantoms in pursuit of a petrified boy in this 1930s Halloween postcard from the USA.

drink. Photos and souvenirs may also be brought out and stories told about those who have passed away. The stories may be funny and entertaining, as well as sad. Families will also clean up the gravestones and decorate them with marigolds, known as 'flowers of the dead'. The marigolds, which are bright orange in colour, are thought to attract the dead spirits to the place where the offerings are made. In addition, people dress up as skeletons in period costume. The female figures are known as Catrinas and have a connection to the ancient goddess, or 'lady of the dead'. They are also inspired by a famous image by Jose Guadalupe Posada of a skeleton dressed as a rich, upper-class woman, which he used to make fun of the ruling elite in Mexico.

GRAVEYARD PICNICS

The offerings on the altars include toys and sweets for the deceased children, and bottles of alcohol such as mescal and tequila for the adults. Food offerings may include skulls made out of sugar, candied pumpkin and sweet buns called 'pan de muerto', which are decorated with pieces of dough resembling bones, shaped in a circle to represent the circle of life, and teardrops to portray the sadness of the loss. The Day of the Dead is celebrated in different ways in various regions, but it is common for family members to spend all night at the gravesides of loved ones, and to have picnics in the graveyard. In addition, people make up poems called 'calaveras' or 'skulls' about their loved ones, or about famous people, and newspapers print cartoons of skeletons. In cities, children dress up and knock on the doors of houses to ask for a 'calaverita', or gift of money or sweets; this custom is similar to that of 'trick or treat' on Halloween night.

In Catholic countries, All Saints Day and All Souls Day, which fall at the same time as the Day of the Dead, are celebrated with public holidays, visits to graveyards and offerings of sweets, candles, flowers, and toys. In the Philippines, the Day of the Dead is celebrated with family reunions. The families camp out in cemeteries, playing card games, eating, drinking, dancing and singing. In Nepal, the dead are celebrated with the 'Cow Pilgrimage', in which families of the deceased lead a cow, or a person dressed as a cow, through the streets. The cow is thought to lead the spirit of the dead into the realm of the afterlife.

The Festivities of Halloween

In the West, Halloween is celebrated on 31 October and is thought to be originally connected to the pagan festival of Samhain. On this night people make 'jack-o'-lanterns', which are pumpkins hollowed out to make the shape of a face, with a small candle inside to give an eerie appearance. In the past, these faces were carved from turnips and represented the souls in purgatory, waiting to go to heaven or hell. In addition, children dress up and go out onto the streets for 'trick or treating'. The children knock on doors and ask 'Trick or treat'? If someone replies 'trick', the children may perform a harmless prank or some other kind of mischief. More commonly, the answer is 'treat', in which case the child is given sweets. Trick or treat activities are thought to have originated in the USA in the 1930s, but there are similar customs that are much older, such as the medieval 'souling', in which poor people would go round the houses asking for food in return for saying prayers for the dead. In Scotland, children may go out 'guising' – to get their treat, they must recite a poem or story or sing a song.

Section Two

REALM OF THE PARANORMAL

CONTACTING THE DEAD

Many people believe they can contact the dead in the afterlife. A medium, a person who claims to have the ability to communicate with the spirits of the deceased, often performs a séance. The séance involves a group of people gathering together with the express purpose of contacting the dead. In many cases, a bereaved person may wish to speak to a loved one who has recently passed away, or it may be that the group simply wishes to summon any spirit, and question them about their existence, both on earth and in the afterlife.

Séance, Paris 1898. A spiritualist group communicate with the spirit world through Italian medium Eusapia Palladino, seated in the centre.

The Rise of Spiritualism

In the West, this belief is known as spiritualism. It may be connected with religious belief, especially Christianity, which teaches the resurrection of the dead. However, in some cases, spiritualists have no systematic religious beliefs; they simply think that all of us continue to live after death in the spiritual world.

The growth of spiritualism as a belief system and practice dates from the mid-19th century. At this period, because of the romantic movement in art and literature, there was a strong interest in the supernatural, the gothic and horror stories of all kinds. It was thought that the spirits of the dead could teach the living about a higher plane of existence, and that they could act as 'spirit guides', giving us moral and practical advice about our lives. It was also believed that the spirits themselves were continuing to develop and improve in the afterlife, so that they came nearer to the state of 'Infinite Intelligence'. 'Infinite Intelligence' is how spiritualists describe God, as a moving force in the universe, expressed through the wonder and beauty of the natural world around us.

RELIGIOUS FRENZY

Spiritualism as a movement, first appeared in upstate New York in the 1840s. Historically, settlers had flocked to the lands that were previously the stronghold of the Iroquois Native Americans, and religious and social radicals had begun to form communities dedicated to new ways of living. These ranged from one extreme to another. For example, there were the Shakers, who advocated celibacy, and in the opposite corner, the Oneida Community, who wanted to establish free love. The region's reputation for religious frenzy, and people who wanted to sweep away the old social order and bring in the new, earned it the name of 'the Burned Over District'.

There were all manner of sects operating in the area at the time, including followers of Jemima Wilkinson, who was thought to be the female reincarnation of Christ; Charles Grandison Finney, a Presbyterian preacher leading a revivalist movement in what became known as 'the Second Great Awakening'; and William Miller, an early pioneer of the Adventist belief in the Day of Judgement. In addition, the Mormon church of the Latter Day Saints was also building up a big following in the region. Because of the number of religious communities in the area, many believed that direct communication with God, angels and ghosts was possible there.

SENSATION AND SHOWMANSHIP

Into this melting pot of evangelical fervour came the spiritualists, who took their cue from earlier writers such as Emanuel Swedenborg and Franz Mesmer. Swedenborg had written about his visions of the afterlife, describing it in detail. He claimed that, rather than a simple heaven or hell, there were a series of planes of existence in the afterlife and that spirits dwelling in these planes can be contacted by the living. Moreover, he taught that the spirits are often conduits for God, being used by Him as a means of communicating to those of us still on earth. Franz Mesmer, for his part, contributed a method of contacting the spirit. He taught that a state of trance could be induced in a person that would render them accessible to contact by supernatural beings. This technique, called Mesmerism, later became known as hypnotism. The early proponents of Mesmerism carried out their public exhibitions with a great deal of showmanship, as did many of the revivalist sects, who made a great spectacle out of baptism rituals and speaking in tongues.

Superstition, necromancy and séance. French colour woodcut, 1850.

THE FOX SISTERS

In 1848, three sisters called Leah, Margaret and Kate Fox, reported that they had heard unexplained rapping, or knocking, sounds in their house at night. The girls responded to it, snapping their fingers and asking the 'spirit' to repeat the number of snaps, which it did. They then developed a system of asking the spirit questions and knocking a certain number of times for 'yes' or 'no'. The girls called the spirit 'Mr Splitfoot', and claimed that it was the ghost of a peddler who had been murdered and buried in the cellar.

PUBLIC SÉANCES

Leah, Kate and Margaret were introduced to members of a radical Quaker group, and the Spiritualist movement was born. The Fox sisters conducted a number of sensational public meetings in which they communicated with the spirits. These meetings were attended by many famous people and encouraged others to take up the practice of 'spirit rapping', as it became known. Within a short time, hundreds of people pronounced themselves 'mediums', that is, individuals gifted with the power to contact the spirit world.

However, some people were sceptical of the girls' claims. A patent official, Charles Grafton, complained that the girls' long skirts made it difficult to detect whether contraptions that could make rapping noises were hidden beneath their garments. Others thought the séances frivolous, and indeed the girls often asked the spirits trivial questions. However, as they grew older, they became more serious. Eventually, Kate's power as a medium was described by a well-known scientist, William Crookes, who said that she had an extraordinary gift:

With mediums, generally it is necessary to sit for a formal séance before anything is heard; but in the case of Miss Fox it seems only necessary for her to place her hand on any substance for loud thuds to be heard in it, like a triple pulsation, sometimes loud enough to be heard several rooms off. In this manner I have heard them in a living tree – on a sheet of glass – on a stretched iron wire – on a stretched membrane – tambourine – on the roof of a cab – and on the floor of a theatre. Moreover, actual contact is not always necessary; I have had these sounds proceeding from the floor, walls, etc., when the

medium's hands and feet were held – when she was standing on a chair – when she was suspended in a swing from the ceiling – when she was enclosed in a wire cage – and when she had fallen fainting on a sofa. I have heard them on a glass harmonicon – I have felt them on my own shoulder and under my own hands. I have heard them on a sheet of paper, held between the fingers by a piece of thread passed through one corner. With a full knowledge of the numerous theories which have been started, chiefly in America, to explain these sounds, I have tested them in every way that I could devise, until there has been no escape from the conviction that they were true objective occurrences not produced by trickery or mechanical means.

SPIRIT KNOCKS OR TOE CRACKING?

Although Kate and Margaret Fox both married wealthy men, their fame and fortune did not last. Over the years, both of them took to drink and eventually fell out with their sister Leah. To upset Leah, who was by now a prominent Spiritualist, they decided to undermine the basis of the movement. On 21 October 1888, Margaret appeared before an audience of 2,000 in New York and demonstrated how she could produce the rapping sound by cracking her toe joints. She later explained in an interview:

My sister Katie was the first to observe that by swishing her fingers she could produce certain noises with her knuckles and joints, and that the same effect could be made with the toes. Finding

that we could make raps with our feet – first with one foot and then with both – we practised until we could do this easily when the room was dark. Like most perplexing things when made clear, it is astonishing how easily it is done. The rapping are simply the result of a perfect

The Fox Sisters of Hydesville, New York. The famous 'Hydesville Rappings' led the girls to perform their mediumship at various séances and meetings in the area. The sisters were a commercial success, and profited from their exhibitions of spirit rappings, also termed 'typtology'. P. T. Barnum brought them to New York City and a wave of spiritualism swept across America.

control of the muscles of the leg below the knee, which govern the tendons of the foot and allow action of the toe and ankle bones that is not commonly known. Such perfect control is only possible when the child is taken at an early age and carefully and continually taught to practice the muscles, which grow stiffer in later years. … This, then, is the simple explanation of the whole method of the knocks and raps.

To the horror of the Spiritualists she had duped, Margaret added:

'A great many people when they hear the rapping imagine at once that the spirits are touching them. It is a very common delusion. Some very wealthy people came to see me some years ago when I lived in Forty-second Street and I did some rappings for them. I made the spirit rap on the chair and one of the ladies cried out: 'I feel the spirit tapping me on the shoulder.' Of course that was pure imagination.'

WICKED BLASPHEMY

Some pointed out that the raps could be heard from different parts of the room, but sceptics put this phenomenon down to suggestibility, citing the fact that when a person is blindfolded, it is often very hard for them to tell the source of the sound.

Not surprisingly, the two sisters were vilified after this damning confession. Both Margaret and Kate apologized profusely for the lies they had perpetrated. Margaret denounced Spiritualism as, 'an absolute falsehood from beginning to end, as the flimsiest of superstitions, the most wicked blasphemy known to the world,' while Kate added, 'I regard Spiritualism as one of the greatest curses that the world has ever known.' It is unclear why the sisters mounted such an attack on Spiritualism. In later years, Margaret regretted her action, but the damage had been done. The two sisters remained outcasts from that time on and lived out the rest of their lives in poverty.

THE PRETTY YOUNG MEDIUM

Despite the debacle of the Fox Sisters, Spiritualism continued to be extremely popular for the next 80 years. It especially appealed to women, giving many a chance to participate in public life, speaking at meetings and sustaining successful careers, in a way that had previously been denied them. They became mediums and 'trance lecturers', often touring the world and addressing large audiences. Many of them were attractive figures, such as Cora L. V. Scott, a beautiful young medium with ringlets whose girlish manner was contrasted with her seriousness when speaking in her 'spirit voice'. Cora was able to communicate with the spirits through speech and writing, giving esoteric lectures on a variety of subjects, which seemed at odds with her appearance. At the age of 16, she married the first of her four husbands, a Mesmerist, Benjamin Hatch, who managed her career in a most cynical way until the marriage ended in recrimination.

ACHSA W. SPRAGUE

Another highly successful female medium was Achsa W. Sprague, who toured extensively on the 'trance lecturer' circuit, and also wrote for the various Spiritualist publications that had now come into being. At the age of 20, she had become seriously ill and credited her recovery to the intervention of the spirits she had contacted. Like many other Spiritualists of the period, who often had connections with the Quaker and other reformist religious movements, Sprague was an advocate of women's rights and also supported the abolition of slavery.

PASCHAL BEVERLY RANDOLPH

As the Spiritualist movement intensified, 'outsiders', such as women and those of mixed race (who were not usually given a platform in public forums), were suddenly allowed into the spotlight. One such medium was Paschal Beverly Randolph, who introduced the practice of what he called 'sex magic'.

Randolph was a descendant of the colonist William Randolph on his father's side, and his mother was of white, Native American, and Malagasy parentage. His mother died when he was young and he was forced to go to sea to earn a living. He travelled the world from a young age, picking up ideas about mysticism and the occult from his voyages in the East, and later beginning a career as a trance medium. In addition, he trained as a doctor, advocating birth control at a time when it was considered illegal to mention the topic in public.

Randolph also set up a group called the Fraternitas Rosae Crucis, an esoteric society linked to medieval theology and the occult. He taught that, on certain occasions, a married couple could use 'sex magic', that is to use sex as part of a ritual in order to achieve a particular desired end. His idea was that sexual energy could be harnessed to transcend reality and create a trance-like state. He wrote:

If a man has an intelligent and loving wife, with whom he is in complete accord, he can work out

the problems [of how to achieve magical results] by her aid. The rite is a prayer in all cases, and the most powerful [that] earthly beings can employ... it is best for both man and wife to act together for the attainment of the mysterious objects sought.

Success in any case requires the adjuvancy of a superior woman. A harlot or low woman is useless for all such lofty and holy purposes, and just so is a bad, impure, passion-driven apology for a man. The woman shall not be one who accepts rewards for compliance; nor a virgin; or under eighteen years of age; or another's wife; yet must be one who hath known man and who has been and still is capable of intense mental, volitional and affectional energy, combined with perfect sexive and orgasmal ability; for it requires a double crisis to succeed...

The entire mystery can be given in very few words, and they are: An upper room; absolute personal, mental, and moral cleanliness both of the man and wife. An observance of the law just cited during the entire term of the experiment

– 49 days. *Formulate the desire and keep it in mind during the whole period and especially when making the nuptive prayer, during which no word may be spoken, but the thing desired be strongly thought...*

Randolph was the first writer to discuss sex magic, an idea that was later taken up by a number of occultists, including Aleister Crowley. A cultured and well-travelled man, Randolph had many powerful friends and acquaintances, including President Abraham Lincoln. However, he met with a violent end, dying at the age of 49. His death was given as suicide by the coroner, but it later emerged that a friend had killed him in a fit of jealousy and insanity.

The Wickedest Man in the World. Aleister Crowley, 1875-1947, English magician, poet, prophet and sex occultist was perhaps one of the most controversial personalities of the 1930s. Like many misunderstood men, Crowley claimed he was a man before his time.

RISE OF THE SÉANCE

The popularity of mediums and trance lecturers like the Fox Sisters increased, helped by the showmanship of the acts. Some of these performances were completely fraudulent, duping the spectators and charging large sums of money for doing so. However, there were others that were completely serious about the endeavour. Spiritualists who claimed they could contact the dead became a major attraction on the touring circuit, and interest in spiritualism increased greatly at the turn of the century.

Private Séances

The word 'séance' means 'session' in French, but in English it came to betoken a particular kind of session, that of a gathering of people trying to contact the spirit world, often through a medium. In the late 19th century, some very well-known people held séances, for example Mary Todd Lincoln, the wife of President Abraham Lincoln, who had suffered the deaths of many members of her family, including her son Willie, and wished to contact them. There were also record attendance figures at public meetings of famous trance lecturers like Paschal Beverly Randolph, but behind the scenes private séances began to take place, in which people would gather to contact their loved ones.

TRANCE MEDIUM

Usually, the séance takes place in a darkened room, where participants sit around a table. The leader of the group, or medium, goes into a trance, the idea being that in this way the spirits will enter the medium's body and speak through them. In other instances, the spirits are said to communicate through a defined number of raps (as with the Fox Sisters). Automatic writing, in which the leader writes messages without, apparently, knowing what they are doing, may also be used. The medium may report going into a trance, receiving the messages from the dead, 'becoming' that person for a while, passing the messages to the living and then coming out of the trance. Often the medium claims to have no memory of what happened while in the trance. Today, this process is sometimes called 'channelling'.

The Ouija Board

A feature of the séance is the ouija board, also known as the 'spirit board' or 'talking board'. Some believe the mysterious-sounding name comes from the French word for yes, 'oui' and its counterpart in Dutch, 'ja'. The ouija board is a flat, often home-made, board, marked with letters, numbers and occult symbols. A small, heart-shaped piece of wood, known as a 'planchette' is used to indicate the letters that the spirit is said to spell out. All the participants in the séance place their fingers lightly on the planchette, which then moves around the board. In some cases, an upside-down glass or other small object may be used for this purpose.

TOOL OF THE OCCULT

The ouija board was commercially manufactured in the late 19th century and from then on came to be seen as a harmless board game. Even so, some Christian sects continued to see it as a powerful tool of the occult. Sceptics, however, put down the movement of the planchette to a phenomenon called the 'ideomotor effect'. This means that subjects are very suggestible and can react by moving parts of their body, such as fingers on a planchette, without being consciously aware that they are doing it. Thus, if our unconscious mind wants us to spell out a message, we do so, because our body sometimes acts without our volition, independently of our conscious thoughts.

How to Hold a Séance

• First, assemble your guests. It is widely held that the number of participants must be divisible by three, but this does not seem to be a hard and fast rule. However, there should be no fewer than three people in the group.

• Make sure that your guests will not be upset or disturbed by the séance. Those of a nervous disposition, or children, should not be invited to a séance.

• Decide which spirit you want to communicate with, usually this will be a recently deceased friend or family member.

• Choose a medium. This could be a person who has held séances before or someone who considers that they have psychic abilities.

• Get a suitable table. The table should be round or oval if possible, since the round table represents the symbolic circle believed necessary for the ritual.

• Lay out your table. In the middle, place some basic food, such as bread or soup. This is believed to help attract the spirits who are only recently dead and who still seek nourishment.

• Also in the middle of the table, place at least three candles (or a number divisible by three). The more candles you place on the table, the more spirits will be attracted, for spirits are said to seek warmth and light.

• The room should be silent, if possible. Never have a radio or television on, or distractions of any kind. Spirits will only enter a quiet, peaceful room.

• Ask your guests to sit around the table. Once they are seated, ask them to join hands in a circle.

• Now summon the spirit. The guests and the medium may wish to speak these words: 'Our beloved [name of spirit], we bring you gifts from life into death. Commune with us (name of spirit), and move among us.'

• Remain silent until there is a response. If none comes, repeat the words until the spirit responds.

• If and when the spirit responds – either by the medium speaking in its voice, or by a series

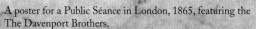
A poster for a Public Séance in London, 1865, featuring the The Davenport Brothers.

THE DAVENPORT BROTHERS'
PUBLIC CABINET SÉANCE.

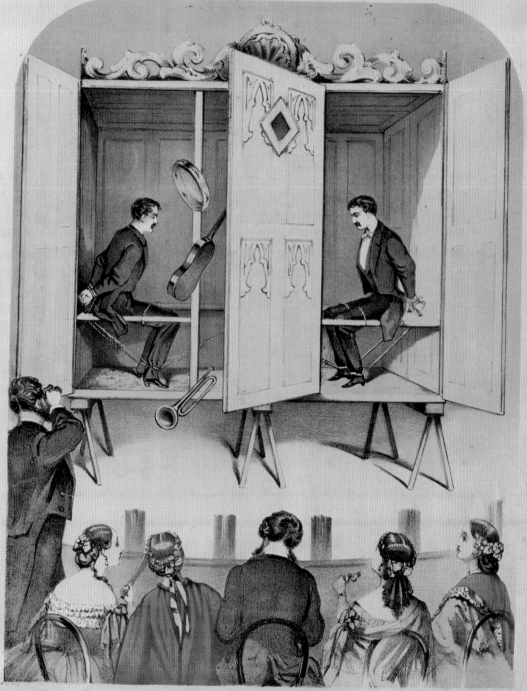

NOW BEING HELD AT

1865

THE QUEEN'S CONCERT ROOMS,
HANOVER SQUARE.

of knocks, you can begin to ask some simple questions.

- Start with questions to which the answer can only be 'yes' or 'no': one rap for no, two raps for yes, for example.

- Next you may be able to ask questions directly to the medium, who may be able to answer in the voice of the spirit you have chosen. Do not ask too many questions and try to make the ones you do ask important. If any of your guests become upset, you can end the séance by breaking the circle of hands, blowing out the candles and turning on the lights.

- When you have finished, thank the spirit for joining you and ask them to go in peace. Break the circle of hands and blow out the candles. Ensure that your guests are feeling calm and help them to calm themselves if they have become disturbed.

A Spooky Séance Experience

A séance is the perfect setting for unusual happenings, so it is no surprise that bizarre stories about them exist. There is a story about a singing group consisting of three young women in the 1950s known as 'The Three Shades'. The women dressed as cowgirls and were part of a troupe of circus performers, including a trick cyclist, a pianist and a double act. They were staying in accommodation next to an ancient church, and decided that evening to hold a séance just for a bit of fun, since there was nothing to do in the sleepy British village where they were stopping for only one night. The troupe joined in, including the trick cyclist, who was very scathing about the whole endeavour and kept making sarcastic remarks.

With the pianist in the role of medium, the séance began. When he asked if there was a spirit present, the candles in the room began to flicker and then went out. The candles were re-lit, whereupon two of the bars on the electric fire in the room changed colour from red to bluish white. When the medium asked the spirit to show another sign of its presence, the door burst open and the room was filled with a scent of flowers.

Encouraged by this success, the group turned to an ouija board and asked for further communication to be made. Despite the fact that they had all linked hands, a loud knocking sound was heard from the table. The planchette on the ouija board then spelt out the following name: Lorenzo de Medici. The spirit of this famous Italian statesman of the 15th century, who was a patron of the arts, announced that the trick cyclist was going to have an accident. The cyclist was unimpressed, since he had not had an accident for many years.

WARNING OF EVIL

Scared and exhausted, the troupe went off to their beds, but as they did, one of them stopped in front of a grandfather clock. Above her, she saw the clock face come loose and crash to the ground at her feet. In terror, she raced off to bed. The three women were so frightened that they crowded into the same bed that night, and in the morning, vowed never to hold a séance again. Some weeks later, the trick cyclist had a nasty fall in his act. When it happened, the others of the troupe remembered the séance and wondered if it had anything to do with the spirit that the cyclist had been so sarcastic about.

The Trumpet Séance

Sometimes a 'trumpet' is used at a séance, which allegedly helps to summon the spirits. The trumpet is usually a simple, lightweight aluminium cone, shaped like a traffic cone. The idea is the spirit will use this cone as an amplifier, so that the spirit – which, of course, lacks vocal cords – can project his or her voice into the room and everybody can hear it. This process is called 'direct voice phenomena'. Since séances are often held in complete darkness, the base of the cone can be painted in fluorescent paint so that the cone can be seen during the session.

Usually a trumpet séance lasts around two to three hours, and involves around 10 to 12 sitters. The sitters are arranged in a semicircle, facing the medium who sits a few feet in front of them, facing the circle. The trumpet is placed between the sitters and the medium. The trumpet must not be touched during the séance as it is believed that, at this time, the trumpet is electrified by a dark force and could cause a shock to the person touching it. Sometimes, one large trumpet is used; in other instances, there may be two or even three, smaller ones. During the session, the cones are said to levitate, according to the level of spiritual energy of the person who is talking at that time. This levitation can be seen because of the ring of fluorescent paint at the bottom of the cone.

THE VOICE OF THE GATEKEEPER

At the start of the séance, the medium goes into a trance. Meanwhile, the sitters may chant or say a prayer, asking for the protection of the spirits. It is believed that once the medium has gone into his or her trance, there should be no loud noises, otherwise the medium may jolt back into his or her own body too fast and cause a shock – some cases allege that mediums have died of shock during this process. Therefore, all concerned are careful to be quiet and not to disturb the medium. When the medium has reached a state of deep trance, the voice of a 'gatekeeper' may be heard. This spirit protects the medium and the circle by allowing only certain spirits to come through, acting as a go-between, or mediator, between the discarnate spirit world and the incarnate physical world. The gatekeeper may ask the assembled company to sing or chant, in order to raise the level of their spiritual vibration so that the voice of the waiting spirits may come through. It is thought to be important for the sitters to keep up a level of engagement, so that the spirits realize that they are being listened to, and do not lose heart or leave.

Sometimes, the sitters will be invited up to the trumpet to collect what is called an 'apport', an object delivered or moved by a spirit. The sitter cups his or her hands under the trumpet and soon hears a clinking noise as the apport comes down the cone. The sitter takes the apport and returns to his or her seat, but usually cannot see it in the dark. The spirit guide may explain what the object is, for example a crystal to help with meditation. In some cases, the departed spirit of a family member will come through, but this is rare. Usually, the trumpet séance is conducted to put members in touch with their 'master spirits', or 'spirit guides', who will help them through their daily lives.

In some cases, individuals may experience highly unpleasant sensations at a séance. For example, they may feel pressure on their heads and shoulders as if someone or something were pressing down on them. They may feel nauseous and their vision may be impaired, with strange distortions. Ringing in the ears may also be heard. Such experiences may lead to later feelings of intense anxiety and it is advised that those who might be affected in this way should not attend séances.

ABOVE: An Edwardian family photo with a ghostly visitor.

RIGHT: Ghostly Parishioner, Alton Church, Staffordshire, England. On 12 September 1993, Eddie Coxon, a local member of the congregation took this photo during a flower festival. Eddie said, 'I swear no one was in front of the camera, and I didn't use a flash. It's a real mystery.'

EXORCIZING THE POSSESSED

Séances, ouija boards and contacting the dead proved so popular that by the early 20th century there was an explosion of claims about ghosts and other paranormal activities. A number of famous people were known to be fascinated by the spirit world, including Arthur Conan Doyle and William Butler Yeats. However, there were also many sceptics, who quickly pointed out the 'showbiz' element of spiritualism — the sensationalist lecture tours, the flamboyant public séances. In order to investigate the claims and counter-claims, a body was set up, the Society for Psychical Research, which still exists today.

HARRY HOUDINI

Investigations into the paranormal were hotly contested in the press of the time. Well-known figures such as Harry Houdini, the escapologist, denounced the mediums as fraudulent and announced, 'Up to the present time everything I have investigated has been the result of deluded brains'. He mounted shows in which he pitted himself against mediums and proved that their tricks were fraudulent, advertised with posters asking, 'Do Spirits Return', to which Houdini replied: 'No', and promised to prove it.

SCIENTISTS CONVERT

Although some mediums were revealed to be completely fraudulent and simply trying to make money out of pretending to summon ghosts,

there were also cases that convinced the investigators. Many scientists who had approached the claims of the spiritualists became converts. These included William James, the pioneering American psychologist, the biologist Alfred Wallace, physicist William Crookes. Harry Price himself, who had successfully investigated and exposed several paranormal occurrences on behalf of the Society for Psychical Research, came to believe in the phenomenon.

TABLE TURNING

Table turning, or 'table tipping' was a form of séance that also became fashionable at around this time. Guests would be invited to seat themselves around a table, usually a round table, and place their hands upon it. In time, the table

Do Spirits Return? A poster for a Harry Houdini show from the 1920s exposing fake spiritualists. The shows cost Houdini the friendship of Sir Arthur Conan Doyle who was a firm believer in spiritualism.

Do Spirits Return?

HOUDINI

SAYS NO - AND PROVES IT
3 SHOWS IN ONE

MAGIC-ILLUSIONS-ESCAPES = FRAUD MEDIUMS EXPOSED

LYCEUM THEATRE
PATERSON
THURS. FRI. SAT. SEPT. 2·3·4

would start to rotate, tipping over to one side. The medium, or another guest, would begin to recite the alphabet and the table would tip to one side when a particular letter came up. In this way, whole words and sentences could be spelt out, which were believed to be communications from the spirit world.

'ECTENIC FORCE'

The phenomenon of table turning, like other spiritualist activities, was carefully investigated by professionals. A French politician named Count Agenor de Gasparin and a Swiss Professor of Natural History at the Academy of Geneva, Monsieur Thury, looked into table turning to try and determine a logical cause for it. The pair explained the movement of the table as the result of what they called 'ectenic force', a form of spiritual energy given off by a medium. This force, they claimed, allows the medium to transport objects without any actual physical contact with them.

The claims about ectenic force were countered by other scientists and commentators, including Dr John Elliotson, who explained it as a type of hypnotism exerted on the sitters. Others, such as surgeon James Braid and physiologist W. B. Carpenter, were convinced that the table turning was caused by the suggestibility of the sitters, while the famous scientist Michael Faraday demonstrated, with the use of some simple experiments, that the table turning took place as a result of unconscious muscular action on the part of the sitters.

The Practice of Exorcism

As well as summoning spirits through séances, humanity has always had a need to banish them, particularly when they are said to inhabit or 'possess' an individual human being. In the West, exorcism became part of the liturgy of the Christian church and continues to be practised to this day. We also find variations on the theme in many other cultures and religions, including Islam, Hinduism and Buddhism.

In the Christian church, ministers are employed to cast out spirits of all kinds, whether demons or poltergeists, from places and people. They do so by invoking the name of Jesus Christ and incanting various prayers, sometimes using incense, icons, amulets and so on. As well as Christ, a number of angels may be called upon to help cast the spirit out. In the case of a possessed person, the idea is that the person themselves is innocent, but needs this help to expel whatever demon is causing them to behave in a destructive, aggressive way.

HOW TO PERFORM AN EXORCISM

Where a poltergeist is active in a house, or a person is behaving as if possessed by a demon, help will be sought from a minister of the church. However, before taking this step it is advisable to find out whether there may be any other cause for the disturbances made by a supposed poltergeist and, in the case of a person possessed, the possibility of mental illness must be ruled out in advance. Performing an exorcism on a person who is suffering from mental illness could prove dangerous and damaging, and the need for medical and psychological help must first be considered.

• The person performing the exorcism, whether a minister or a layperson, must have faith in their power to command the demons. This may be religious faith, or simply a knowledge of the paranormal, and a belief in the ability to control the situation.

• A set of prayers must be recited. In the Christian faith, these will begin with an appeal to God to help cast out the demon from the place or person. In other faiths, a higher power will be invoked and a number of demands made, asking the devil to leave.

• The minister must make the sign of the cross at the appropriate times during the prayers. Signing of the cross must be made on the minister himself, as the exorcist, and the subject.

• The sprinkling of holy water on the room, the furniture and everyone in the room, is another practice designed to exorcize the evil spirit. Among Catholics, the subject may be touched with a holy relic.

• Finally, it is expected that the demon will somehow reveal itself. This may be in a number of ways. In the case of a poltergeist, objects around the house may be thrown and broken. In the case of a possessed person, the subject may howl and scream, writhe about, or otherwise act as if in extreme pain. This is because the evil spirit

will be unwilling to leave its home, and will put up a fight before it departs.

AN ANCIENT FORMULA

The following is an ancient formula for exorcism, based on that of the early Coptic Christian church. Firstly, there should be some preparations. Seven small olive branches should be gathered together. Six of these must be tied together, while the seventh is used as a whip during the proceedings. Secondly, the branches must be placed in front of the possessed person. Thirdly, a liturgy is recited over him or her, as follows:

Hail God of Abraham!
Hail God of Isaac!
Hail God of Jacob!
Jesus the righteous
Holy Spirit
Son of the Father,
  below the seven
  within the seven
Come!

Direct your power to (here, speak the person's name)
Drive Satan, this unclean demon within him, away
I command you, demon, whoever you may be, by the power of
Come out, demon, whoever you may be
Stay away from (speak the person's name)
Quickly! Now! Come out, demon!
I bind you with unbreakable chains of adamantine!
I cast you into the abyss of hell!

Finally, once the exorcism is completed, an amulet should be hung on the sufferer with a relevant prayer, to make sure that the demon stays away.

Devil expulsion. The exorcism of a woman possessed by demons. 16th century woodcut.

THE CANHAM FAMILY - the UK's foremost ghost hunting family. While most of us prefer to go and see a scary film for thrills, the Canham family prefer to explore ancient buildings in the middle of the night. Mother Wendy, 37, father Gary, 44 and daughter Nikki, 16, spend their evenings in underground tunnels hoping to meet spirits. Nikki - who began ghost hunting aged just 14 - is thought to be the UK's youngest ghosthunter. These 'Light orbs' were captured by Gary at Coalhouse Fort, Tilbury, Essex, England in 2010.

ROBBIE MANNHEIM

Robbie Mannheim, also known as Roland Doe, was the pseudonym of a man who was allegedly possessed by the devil, and underwent an exorcism while still a child in the 1940s. Since the real identity of the man is unknown, most of the facts surrounding the case come from the testimony of a priest, Father Raymond Bishop, who kept a diary of what happened, and Rev. Walter H. Halloran, who also participated in the exorcism.

Robbie Mannheim was born into a Lutheran family in Cottage City, Maryland. An only child, he spent a good deal of his time with his Aunt Harriet, who was a spiritualist. Disregarding the rules against involving children in summoning the dead, his aunt introduced him to the ouija board at a young age. Apparently, when she died, he attempted to contact her via the ouija board at a séance, thus – in the view of some commentators – causing him to become possessed by an evil spirit.

INSPIRATION FOR
THE EXORCIST

When Robbie's aunt died, a poltergeist began to make its presence felt around the house. Furniture shifted around of its own accord, objects such as vases flew across the rooms, and there were sounds of marching feet. Then Robbie himself began to be affected. The word 'hell' appeared pricked out on his skin, and when a vial of holy water was placed next to him, it smashed into pieces. In a panic, Robbie's family contacted their local priest, who arranged for Robbie to sleep at his house so that he could observe him. During the night, the priest heard scratching noises, saw an armchair tilting up, and witnessed other strange events. He decided to have the boy exorcized at the local Jesuit hospital, where his behaviour became extremely disturbed. Robbie attacked one minister, and when he was sent home, defecated on the walls of the house and began to speak in a strange, guttural voice. He was exorcized again, over 30 times, this time by several priests, who described various happenings, such as the word 'evil' appearing on his skin. Eventually, in the final exorcism, there was a loud thunderclap and Robbie allegedly remarked, 'It's over.' Robbie returned home, where he proceeded to live a normal life, untroubled by further problems. His case later inspired the film *The Exorcist*, released in 1973.

ANNELIESE MICHEL

One of the most shocking exorcism cases in recent times was that of Anneliese Michel, a girl born in Leiblfing, Bavaria, in 1952. In her short life she experienced 67 exorcisms at the hands of two priests, and no one can say for sure if the devil was really driven out of her.

Fits and Evil Voices

As a child, she was raised as a devout Catholic and took her religion very seriously. When she was a teenager, she would make reparation for the sins of others by sleeping on a cold, bare floor in the middle of winter. In 1969, when she was 17, she began to suffer from epileptic fits. Then she reported that, when she began to pray, voices would tell her that she was going to 'stew in hell'. She began to suffer depression and thought of suicide to end her miserable existence. Her behaviour became disturbed. She would drink her own urine off the floor, eat spiders and coal, and tear at her clothes. She was taken to psychiatrists and treated, but with no success.

DEMONIC POSSESSION

At the age of 23, Anneliese set out on a pilgrimage, and on the way met a woman who told her that she was suffering from demonic possession. They found an exorcist in a nearby town and gained permission from the bishop of the church to perform the rite.

Between 1975 and 1976, a total of 67 exorcisms were carried out, at the rate of one or two a week. Some of these rituals were lengthy, lasting up to four hours. Over this period, Anneliese's health began to deteriorate; she starved herself, hoping that in this way the devil would depart from her soul. She also hoped to atone for the sins of the younger generation, whom she regarded as depraved, and for priests who had committed various crimes.

DEATH FROM MALNUTRITION

However, the only effects were that Anneliese became increasingly disturbed and physically weaker. During the year that the exorcisms were carried out, she was no longer being taken to the doctor, and had given up hope that medical intervention could help her. On July 1976, Anneliese Michel died in her sleep of malnutrition and dehydration. She weighed only 68 pounds. After her death, the state prosecuted two priests involved in the case, Father Ernst Alt and Father Arnold Renz, together with her parents. They were charged

with neglectful homicide. Anneliese's body had to be exhumed for the investigation and tapes of the exorcisms were played to the court. In the end, both the priests and her parents were found guilty, but were all given suspended sentences.

THE TRUTH EMERGES

During her lifetime, Anneliese claimed that she had been possessed by many demons, including those of Lucifer, Judas Iscariot, Nero, Cain, Hitler and a man named Fleischmann, a disgraced priest from the 16th century. She also claimed to see the faces of demons on people and objects around her. At the height of her illness, she began to speak in an inhuman, growling voice very like that of the character Linda Blair in the film, *The Exorcist*, which was released in 1973. This has led some commentators to believe that Anneliese was influenced by the film and that in her mental distress she took on the identity of the character. When details of the trial came to light, it emerged that neither the priests nor the parents of the young woman had contacted a doctor when she began to refuse food. Had they hospitalized her, it would have been possible to save her life through force feeding. For this reason, they were charged with neglect. In addition, when she was very weak, they continued the exorcisms, making her genuflect, or bow, over and over again, so often that the ligaments in her knees ruptured.

NEGLECTFUL HOMICIDE

Other disturbing facts came to light during the trial. It emerged that Anneliese's mother had given birth to an illegitimate daughter, Martha, before her wedding day and as a result, had been forced to wear a black veil. Her mother encouraged Anneliese to perform atonement rituals for the sinful birth of her sister Martha. Sadly, when Martha died at the age of eight during an operation for a kidney tumour, Anneliese took it upon herself to increase the penances. As a teenager, this idea of atoning for the sins of others took on a central role in her life, and she began to adopt all kinds of other penances for people unknown to her. In addition, the role of the priests may have exacerbated her psychotic tendencies. Both the priests explained to her that she was possessed by a demon. The exorcism rites themselves reinforced this idea, to the point that Anneliese felt she was no longer in control of her actions, but inhabited by a powerful evil force. For this reason, she became more and more mentally disturbed until she died.

After the trial, some prominent German Roman Catholics petitioned the church in Rome to have the exorcism rite altered to stop this happening again. In January 1999, the Catholic Church revised the Rite of Exorcism, although the traditional rite is still legal if it is performed in Latin. The new ritual emphasizes that a possessed person continues to hold free will, although their physical actions may be controlled by an evil spirit. In practice, Catholic bishops rarely authorize exorcisms today and prefer to direct people asking for it to the medical services, believing that a diagnosis of mental illness or epilepsy is more likely in all cases.

In 2005, the story of Anneliese Michel loosely formed the basis of a film, *The Exorcism of Emily Rose*, which was met with opposition from the Michel family. Another film, *Requiem*, directed by Hans-Christian Schmid, was released in 2006. This German-language film was much more closely based on the true events of the case.

The Exorcism of Emily Rose, 2005. When the director, Scott Derrickson, found out that Jennifer Carpenter (pictured) is double jointed, he decided that the positions she was able to contort herself into were far more unsettling than could be accomplished with a dummy, so Carpenter did many of the exorcism stunts herself.

GHOST HUNTING

Paranormal investigation, or ghost hunting, is a popular activity today, as evidenced by the many reality TV shows dedicated to exploring places that are thought to be haunted. Ghost hunting teams set out to find evidence of ghostly activity using high-tech equipment such as camera and video equipment, sound recorders and an EMF meter. This instrument measures electromagnetic fields, as ghosts are said to alter electromagnetic energy, and can apparently be detected this way. Geiger counters, which measure fluctuations in radiation, may also be used.

THE LONDON GHOST CLUB

As well as making a thorough scientific investigation of the site, ghost hunters like to collect evidence regarding the history of the place where the haunting is said to occur. This will involve interviewing local people and researching the events that have taken place in the area, often looking through documents and historical records for clues. Some paranormal investigators will bring along a trance medium, clairvoyant or psychic; these individuals are believed to have special powers making them sensitive to the presence of the dead. In some cases, church ministers or others will be brought along to perform an exorcism, or to advise on how best to rid the area of the ghost.

In recent years, ghost hunting has become more popular, largely owing to media coverage in such films as *Ghostbusters*, as well as reality TV shows such as *Ghost Hunters* and *Most Haunted*.

There are businesses that trade in ghost-hunting equipment, and groups have been set up that make tours in allegedly haunted areas. In the past, there were also societies specializing in ghost hunting, including The Ghost Club, founded in London in 1862, which is still operating. This club first became active during the era when spiritualism was a growing movement and had many famous members, including novelists Charles Dickens and Arthur Conan Doyle, and poets W. B. Yeats and Siegfried Sassoon. One prominent member was the ghost hunter Harry Price, who had made his name with his book on the haunting of Borley Rectory (see page 83-6).

FACT OR FICTION?

Today, ghost hunter groups continue to thrive; in fact, there has been a boom in the popularity in the last two decades. In October 2008, a poll conducted by Associated Press and Ipsos found

that 34 per cent of Americans claimed to believe in ghosts. The technology has become more complex, with improved methods of measuring cold spots, orbs of light, unusual noises and electromagnetic fields. However, most scientists dismiss the findings of these groups, saying that their methods are not scientific. Their evidence is usually flawed, since most of their readings can be attributed to random variations in the environment, caused by all sorts of phenomena

Harry Price, the ghost hunter, in his own faked 'ghost' photo, showing how the fraud photographer William Hope created his spirit album photographs by using multiple exposure techniques to render the appearance of ghostly apparitions.

other than ghosts (for example, radio signals, dust particles and faulty wiring).

Interestingly, not all ghost hunter groups have members who are fully convinced of the existence of ghosts. In some cases, there are sceptics who are not persuaded one way or the other and want to find out, through scientific methods and rational argument, whether there is any evidence to cause us to believe that spirits of the dead may haunt a place or communicate with living human beings.

Harry Price: Psychic Researcher

Harry Price was one of the first ghost hunters to become well known in the 1920s, when his exploits attracted the attention of the media. An amateur conjuror, he became a member of the Magic Circle early on in his career. In 1922, he conducted an exposé of a photographer named William Hope, who had treated some photographs to look as if a spirit or ghost was present. In 1934, he formed the University of London Council for Psychical Investigation and the same year began research into the case of the trance medium Helen Duncan. Duncan was famous for summoning the spirits of the dead and emitting ectoplasm, a substance believed to be the physical manifestation of a ghost or spirit, from her mouth.

ON TRIAL FOR WITCHCRAFT

Helen Duncan was paid £50 to offer herself as a subject for the National Laboratory of Psychical Research. The laboratory had previously investigated her 'ectoplasm' and found it to be made of egg white. Price now went on to find that the spirit manifestations that appeared to emanate from her mouth were made of cheesecloth that she had swallowed and then regurgitated. In 1944, Duncan went on to be tried for witchcraft and Price gave his results as evidence for the prosecution. The unfairness of her trial was thought to be a factor in the repeal of the Witchcraft Act of 1735, which was, by the 20th century, completely outmoded. Duncan served a jail term of nine months, after which time, the act was repealed. After Duncan's sentencing, Winston Churchill complained to the Home Secretary about the waste of court resources on the case and the 'obsolete tomfoolery' of the charge.

Price continued his investigations with a number of individuals, including an Indian fire walker, Kuda Bux, seeking to establish the veracity of their claims. He was generally sceptical of those who professed to have supernatural powers, or claimed to be able to contact the dead. As President of the London Ghost Club, he gathered together a group of sceptics who were genuinely interested in discovering the truth about ghosts, telepathy and other aspects of the paranormal. However, his most famous work was *The Most Haunted House in England*, where he claimed that Borley Rectory was indeed haunted by a poltergeist, and that all his tests and experiments there over a period of years pointed to this conclusion.

GHOST TOURS

One of the offshoots of the TV ghost hunter craze has been the growth of 'ghost tours'. All around the world, but particularly in the US and the UK, both private and state-funded tours are available. The tours may visit famous sites including, in the UK, Pendle Hill, a place in Lancashire said to be haunted by demons and spirits, and in the US, the *Queen Mary* ship at Long Beach, California and Whaley House in San Diego, California – to name but a few (see Section Three, Ghostly Legends, page 71).

UFOs, CRYPTIDS AND REVENANTS

As well as ghosts and spirits, there are other kinds of phenomena that have fascinated and puzzled humanity from the dawn of time. These are happenings that cannot be explained by science, and that cannot be understood or investigated by rational explanation or scientific methodology. Indeed, the word 'paranormal' means 'against' or 'beyond' what is considered normal, everyday reality.

Unidentified Flying Objects

The possibility that life exists on other planets in the solar system has long been considered by astrologers, scientists and religious thinkers. It seems to be deep in the human psyche to look up at the stars and wonder what other beings may exist out there. There are many scientific theories, aided by an ever-advancing technology of space investigation, that seek to determine whether intelligent life exists outside our planet. However, what most scientists reject is the idea that 'unidentified flying objects' (UFOs) exist, and that they are flown by alien races visiting or passing by planet Earth. Nevertheless, many claim to have seen these objects, and a belief in them, as well as controversy about their existence, continues to be a constant source of fascination to the general public to this day.

In the 1950s, 'ufologists', as they called themselves, tried to take a scientific approach to investigating tales of flying saucers. In addition, government agencies researched such sightings, often from a military perspective, to gather intelligence about possible threats. Others, such as spiritualists and occultists, sought to prove extra-terrestrial visitations as part of their general belief system about the spirit world. In both cases, it was thought that the UFOs had special powers, were not subject to the ordinary laws of physics, and obeyed different norms. This was consistent with the idea that on other planets, different physical laws (such as the law of gravity) might hold sway.

GHOST ROCKETS AND FOO FIGHTERS

Reports of UFO sightings generally turn out to be aeroplanes, air balloons and meteors. However, in a small percentage of cases, there seems to be no rational explanation for them. One of the most commonly seen objects is the 'flying saucer' (a term coined by pilot Kenneth Arnold in 1947). Arnold reported seeing crescent-shaped aircraft in the sky. Later, the term UFO was adopted by

the United States Air Force to cover all kinds of flying objects of different shapes and sizes.

From ancient times, observers have reported seeing strange objects flying in the sky, and often interpreted them as omens of religious significance. In Western culture, there has been increasing interest in this phenomenon since the early 20th century, when a number of pilots have reported seeing such objects as circular shapes 'like manhole covers', 'wingless cylinders', 'huge ovals' and 'foo fighters' (metallic balls of light) and 'ghost rockets' flying at great speed through the sky, sometimes even forcing the pilots to change direction to avoid collision. The number of UFO reports, and the fact that they came from apparently sensible military sources, gave cause for research, but many continued to claim that the sightings were the result of naturally occurring phenomena, such as light bouncing off clouds, or possibly due to mass delusions in times of stress, such as during battles in the air. For example, a trick of the light known as 'Fata Morgana', in which objects are reflected, appear upside down, or distorted in some way, could be the explanation for seeing what looks like a UFO. There are certain cloud formations, known as lenticular clouds, which have a round shape and could, in some weather conditions, resemble a flying saucer, hence their nickname, 'saucer clouds'.

Whatever the truth of the matter, most governments today no longer spend time and money on researching the phenomenon of UFOs. In 2009, the British government closed down its UFO unit, issuing the following explanation:

In over fifty years, no UFO report has revealed any evidence of a potential threat to the United Kingdom. The MoD has no specific capability for identifying the nature of such sightings. There is no Defence benefit in such investigation and it would be an inappropriate use of defence resources. Furthermore, responding to reported UFO sightings diverts MoD resources from tasks that are relevant to Defence.

It is significant that the government did not dismiss the possibility that UFOs exist; instead, it pointed out that the UFOs, should they exist, have posed no security threat to the country and are therefore not dangerous.

LOW-FLYING BLACK TRIANGLES

Today, the consensus is that most apparent UFO sightings are in fact genuine errors, in which the viewer sees an aircraft, heavenly body or weather pattern, and mistakes it for an alien spaceship. Very few are actual hoaxes. However, between 5 and 20 per cent of sightings cannot be explained in any rational way. These include a number of low-flying black triangles spotted over Belgium between 1989 and 1990; traces of apparent UFO aircraft landings – indentations in the earth, strange magnetic fields, traces of unusual metals and crop circles found in fields and forests; and all kinds of photographic evidence, as well as radar tracking of flying objects in the sky.

To date, these mysteries have not been solved. Some people believe that science is not yet sophisticated enough to explain the movements of objects that may be subject to physical laws of a universe other than our own; some that there must be rationale behind these sightings, but it has not yet been found. Some believe that alien beings from other planets, or spirits from the world of the occult, are indeed visiting us and that their presence should be acknowledged, whether or not they mean us harm.

The Existence of Cryptids

Cryptids are types of animals that are not catalogued by zoologists as existing on earth. These

include legendary monsters such as the Loch Ness Monster from Scotland, Bigfoot from the Pacific Northwest of the USA, the Yeti or Abominable Snowman from the Himalayas and various types of werewolf from different parts of Europe. Other cryptids include two creatures from the US, a dragon-like animal known as the Jersey Devil, from New Jersey and the Mothman, from West Virginia, and from Mexico, the Chupacabra, a kangaroo-like creature that is said to kill and eat goats.

THE MYSTERY OF BIGFOOT

Sightings of Bigfoot, also known as Sasquatch, were first reported in the 19th century, in parts of Washington, Oregon, California, Canada and Alaska. The creature was said to be huge, nearly 8ft (2.4m) tall, and covered in thick brown fur. It was sometimes seen in families, with what seemed to be a mother, father and children. In addition, trackers have alleged that large footprints in snow or soft ground are evidence of the existence of this mysterious creature.

Bigfoot is said not to wear any clothes, not to speak a language and not to use tools. It is thought to be a primitive being, who only communicates by a series of simple calls. The explanations for the existence of such a creature are various; some people believe it is a throwback to prehistoric times when the creature mated with a Neanderthal to create the Bigfoot of today; other people suggest that it is an animal not yet catalogued by zoologists.

THE LOCH NESS MONSTER

Another enduring mystery is that of the Loch Ness Monster, affectionately known as Nessie. This creature is said to have a 'sleek, rubbery, blackish-grey skin' and measures roughly 20ft (6.1m) long. Many visitors to the loch claim to have witnessed the monster, and in some cases, have photographed their findings. Theories

abound as to what the monster is. Some suggest that it may be an extremely large sea serpent living in the loch. Others claim that it is a zeuglodon, a type of primitive whale with horns. To date, the mystery has not been solved and the possibility of catching a glimpse of Nessie continues to be a tourist attraction in the area.

THE WEREWOLF

Werewolves, otherwise known as Lycons, have been seen in many cultures across the world for centuries. Stories about them are particularly prevalent in Europe, where legend has it they are human beings who have transformed into wolves, often through evil, supernatural powers. A number of myths are attached to them, such as that they can only make this transformation during a full moon, and that they can only be killed by a silver bullet. According to cryptozoologists, who attempt to explain the existence of cryptids like these, werewolves may be an unknown species of wild dog, or alternatively a type of Bigfoot that has been mistaken for a wolf.

VAMPIRIC CREATURES

Most cryptozoologists discount the existence of vampires, since they do not believe that human beings can transform themselves into vampires at night and search for human blood to ensure their survival. As far as they are concerned, this is the stuff of folklore and mythology, holding psychological rather than scientific significance for humanity in general. However, cryptozoologists are interested in the possibility that vampiric animals exist and will conduct research into sightings of legendary creatures such as the Chupacabra. As they point out, in actual fact, many creatures live on blood, including leeches, mosquitoes and vampire bats, but to date, it seems unlikely that a blood-sucking legendary creature such as a vampire actually exists in reality.

Section Three

GHOSTLY LEGENDS

WINDSOR CASTLE

Windsor castle was built in the 11th century under the reign of William I. Since that time, and to the present day, it has been the residence of the ruling monarchy. Windsor Castle, one of the oldest buildings in England, is not just known for its history and architecture, but also its ghosts. It is renowned for being one of the most haunted buildings in the world, and what makes the ghost sightings at Windsor castle so unique is that they have included sightings of royal ghosts, such as King Henry VIII, Queen Elizabeth I and King Charles I.

Henry VIII

One of the most commonly sighted ghosts of Windsor Castle is that of Henry VIII. The Tudor King, who is famous for his beheadings, haunts the grounds. Henry VIII was one of many royals to be buried at Windsor castle; he and his third wife Jane Seymour were buried in a vault in St George's chapel. The Tudor King has been seen walking the hallways of Windsor and his groans and shouts have been heard in the Cloisters. His footsteps have also been heard in the hallways as has the sound of him dragging his ulcerated leg. The agonizing screams of Henry VIII have led some theorists to believe that his earthbound spirit is trapped in the castle, forever tormented by the pain that he had inflicted on others.

However, King Henry VIII is not the only Tudor ghost who has been spotted on the castle's grounds. His second wife Anne Boleyn has also been seen at the window of the Dean's Cloister. Anne Boleyn's marriage to Henry VIII changed the course of history enabling men to divorce and remarry. The King ordered her execution after she failed to give him a male heir. It was her untimely, traumatic death that many believe causes her restless spirit to haunt Windsor Castle's grounds. Her ghostly figure has been spotted on numerous occasions looking pale and dismal. The sightings of Anne's ghost were not limited to Windsor castle; she has also been seen at Blickling Hall and the Tower of London, some of the sightings being truly disturbing. For example, Anne Boleyn has been seen sitting in a carriage holding her severed head. The eerie carriage was being pulled by headless horses, spurred by a headless horseman. This was a fearful image for those who witnessed it.

Herne the Hunter

The most famous non-royal ghost to have been spotted on the grounds of Windsor Castle is that of Herne the Hunter who has been associated with Windsor forest for centuries and is believed to be one of the huntsmen of King Richard II. The true cause of his death is unknown but there has been much speculation and circulating stories. Some believe that he had great skill as a huntsman and was favoured by the King. The story states that Herne won the King's favour when he saved the King from being killed by a stag, a rescue which left Herne injured. The King marked Herne as his chief keeper which enraged the other keepers. In jealousy, his colleagues framed him for theft which resulted in Herne hanging himself in the

Herne the Hunter appears to Henry VIII on the terrace of Windsor Castle in the midst of a storm.

forest. Other stories connect Herne to witchcraft and dark magic. The oak tree in Windsor forest where Herne hung himself was renamed 'Herne's oak', and after his death, the hanging body was said to have disappeared, leaving only his spirit to roam the forest.

SYMBOL OF DOOM

After Herne's death, people have seen him haunt the vicinity around Herne's oak and also around the forest. The difference between his ghost sightings and the others at Windsor is that he was not seen as a solemn phantom bound to the grounds, but more of a malevolent spectre. The appearance of the ghost was seen as a sign of impending doom and any hardship in the surrounding area was connected to Herne's ghost. Other people believe that the appearance of his ghost brings misfortune to the royal family. In the 1860s, Herne's oak was felled on an order from Queen Victoria. She asked for the tree to be cut into logs which she later burnt to try and cleanse the Windsor grounds of Herne's spirit. However, her efforts were in vain as the ghost has been seen many times since. Herne's dwelling spirit has haunted the Windsor grounds for many years and has brought about great interest from the public. Even William Shakespeare commented on the famous spectre in his play, *The Merry Wives of Windsor*.

Famous Sightings

Queen Elizabeth I has been said to haunt the royal library by members of the royal family. Her footsteps were usually heard on the floorboards before she was seen walking in her high heels through the library and into another room. Her ghost was said to be dressed in a black dress with a long black, lace shawl covering her shoulders.

Her ghost's sightings were not just confined to the library though; she was also seen at the Dean's Cloister window. Before his death, King George III was confined in his room during his famous battle with dementia, at which time he would peer out of the window at the guards. After his death, his ghost was seen doing the same. He, like many other royal ghosts of Windsor, was buried in the grounds.

A GHOST IN EVERY ROOM

Many rooms within Windsor castle have been reported as being haunted. The Deanery is believed to be haunted by a young boy who shouts out: 'I don't want to go riding today'. Light footsteps have also been heard in the room which has been connected to the same boy. Sir George Villiers has been rumoured to haunt one of the castles bedrooms. In the prison room, children have witnessed a civil war prisoner walking around and adults have felt him brush past them. Bells in the Curfew Tower have been known to start swinging on their own. At times, footsteps were heard on the Curfew Tower staircase before the bells started to swing mysteriously. The Long Walk is haunted by a young guard who had shot himself whilst on duty. Shortly before his suicide, the guard reported seeing paranormal activity and after his death, two guards saw his apparition roaming around the Long Walk. The dead guard's ghost was smiling in both sightings. The ghost of Charles I was also famously spotted in the castle looking spookily similar to his portrait. The sightings have been recorded over the years not just from staff and visitors but also from members of the royal family. The numerous accounts of ghost sightings confirm Windsor to be one of the most haunted castles in the world and a chilling abode for the royals.

TOWER OF LONDON

The historic Tower of London, on the north bank of the River Thames, has long been thought to be haunted by ghosts. Its most famous ghost is that of Anne Boleyn, the second of King Henry VIII's wives, who was beheaded there for treason in 1536. According to the legend, she haunts the chapel of St Peter ad Vincula in the Tower, where she lies buried. She has been seen on many occasions walking the corridors of the Tower at night, with her head tucked under her arm.

Witchcraft, Adultery, Incest and Treason

Anne Boleyn was unpopular as queen during her reign because the public disapproved of the king's behaviour in leaving his first wife for her. King Henry VIII's marriage to Boleyn was also the cause of England's split from the Pope and the Roman Catholic Church, which had great political and religious significance for the country, and caused many bloody disputes. However, the public became more supportive of Boleyn when she fell foul of the king, having failed to produce a male heir to the throne. Disappointed with his new wife, Henry quickly moved his affections to a new woman, Jane Seymour. To get rid of Boleyn and marry Seymour, Henry accused Boleyn of witchcraft, of adultery with five men, all of whom were executed, and of incest with her own brother. She was then stripped of all her privileges, imprisoned in the tower, and finally, executed. Historians believe it to be most unlikely that she committed these crimes, but at her beheading she did not speak out against the king – neither did she admit that she had committed any crime. It is thought that this was in order to protect her daughter, who later became Elizabeth I of England.

THE QUEEN OF DARKNESS?

Some believe the reason Anne Boleyn met her death bravely, wearing a red petticoat and a gown trimmed with ermine, was because she was a witch, and was looking forward to meeting the Prince of Darkness. Before she died, she wrote the following poem:

Oh Death Rock me asleep
Bring on my quiet rest
Let pass my very guiltless ghost
Out of my careful breast
Ring out the doleful knell

75

Let it sound
My death tell
For I must die.

After her death, a number of rumours grew about her, including the famous myth that she had six fingers on one hand, an abnormality which was believed at the time to be a sign of evil. However, when her body was exhumed in 1876, no such abnormalities were discovered. Today, it is thought that these rumours were put about by pro-Roman Catholic writers to discredit the Anglican church, which Henry had founded after his split with Rome.

THE HEADLESS GHOST

The ghost of Anne Boleyn is reputed to haunt the Tower and remains one of the most potent legends of this historical landmark today. Over the centuries there have been numerous sightings of the ghost, all giving different accounts of how she looked and what happened when the witnesses met her. In 1880, a guard told of seeing a light shining inside the church. The guard mounted a ladder and peered into the window. Inside, he saw the church full of people dressed in Elizabethan costume, who moved down the aisle emitting a ghostly light. At the front was a richly dressed woman who looked like Anne Boleyn. As he watched, the whole procession vanished, and the church went dark again. In another instance, a guard had a fatal heart attack, dying of fright after meeting the headless ghost of Anne Boleyn on the staircase. A soldier at the tower also claimed, when he was found asleep on duty, that he had fainted after meeting a woman 'wearing a queer-looking bonnet with no head in it'. He claimed that he had charged at the apparition with his bayonet, but the bayonet had gone right through the body, leaving only a 'fiery flash' that ran up his arm and gave him a shock.

Most of the subsequent reports of meeting the headless ghost were made by guards at the Tower, but it must be added that in some cases, these accounts were given to excuse the offence of falling asleep on duty, and thus avoid being court-martialled for failing to keep watch adequately.

HEADLESS DRIVER AND TEAM OF HORSES

At Blickling Hall in Norfolk, where Anne Boleyn's family once resided, her ghost is said to arrive every year on the 19 May, the anniversary of her death. Her coach arrives at the hall, drawn by headless horses and a headless horseman. The horseman has her severed head in his lap, and it is covered in blood. Anne alights, enters the hall, and walks up and down the corridors until dawn, at which time she vanishes.

At Hever Castle in Kent, where the Boleyn family also lived during her childhood and where Henry courted her in the gardens, a ghostly funeral carriage appears at Christmas time, driving recklessly up the path. As at Blickling, the carriage is drawn by a team of headless horses. A similar visitation occurs at Rochford Hall, Essex, where Anne also lived as a child. Her ghost has also been rumoured to stare glumly out of the window at Windsor Castle, one of the royal residences that she would have lived in when she was Queen of England.

The Grim Prison

The Tower of London has long been associated with the gruesome, bloody events surrounding the successive monarchs of England. When the Normans invaded England in 1066, they built the Tower of London as a royal residence. It was constructed with two sets of defensive walls and a moat, and for this reason served the monarchy

The Beheading of Qg: Anne B

Famous Tower of London Ghosts

well, not only as a place of safety for themselves, but also to incarcerate their enemies – who were many and various. Given its grim role as a prison, where many acts of torture and execution took place, it soon became a symbol of oppression for the people of the country, and has remained a potent symbol of the ruthlessness and violence of the monarchs in English history. In the reign of Queen Elizabeth I, its reputation as a place of torture and imprisonment increased; 'Good Queen Bess', plagued by insurrection on all sides and desperate to hold on to her throne, would order any political opponent to be 'sent to the tower', either to languish there for years, or to meet a violent end at the hands of her henchmen.

The people who were incarcerated in the Tower of London are famous people who played an important part in the history of England. Many were violently interrogated and tortured. Many were sentenced without a trial. Those who were executed had their lives ended with a violent, untimely and tragic death. Countless victims were executed publicly on Tower Hill, just outside the Tower of London by beheading. This barbaric form of execution was common in Medieval and Renaissance England and explains why so many ghosts are sighted in a headless state. Stories of ghosts incarcerated in dungeons explain the 'rat-

Anne Boleyn kneeling on the scaffold before her execution at the Tower of London in 1536. Unfortunately the illustrator's research has let him down: although the executioner is pictured wielding an axe, Anne was executed by sword.

tling of chains' and the terrified shrieks, groans, moans, wails and desperate cries of prisoners account for the noises associated with ghosts.

Executions by Beheading – Showing the head to the crowd

Following execution the severed head was held up by the hair by the executioner. This was done, not as many people think to show the crowd the head, but to show the head the faces in the crowd and its own body! Killing by beheading is not immediate. Consciousness remains for at least eight seconds after beheading until lack of oxygen causes unconsciousness and eventually death.

Traitors' Gate

The Traitors' Gate was the watergate entrance for prisoners condemned after trial at Westminster. It dates from 1240 when Henry III enlarged the fortress by building extra defence works. There is a story that when the work was nearing completion on St George's day 1240 there was a great storm that resulted in the foundations being undermined and the gate collapsing. When the circumstances were repeated identically a year later an inquiry revealed that a priest claimed to have seen the ghost of Archbishop Thomas Becket striking the walls with a giant crucifix. The ghost was proclaiming that the new building was not for the common good but 'for the injury and prejudice of Londoners, my brethren'. Since it was the King's grandfather, Henry II, who had caused the death of the saint he felt it was wise to include a small oratory in the tower of the new building dedicated to Becket. Even so its rooms have always had a reputation of being haunted.

Doors open and close without reason, the figure of a monk in a brown robe has been seen and ghostly footsteps including the distinctive slap of monastic sandals are sometimes heard.

Kings, Noblewomen and a Bear

Other ghosts said to haunt the tower include Henry VI, reputedly a quiet, gentle man who suffered periods of insanity and who was not suited to the bitter struggle for power of the English monarchy. Henry VI had been imprisoned in the tower and died there, possibly murdered by his successor Edward IV. Lady Jane Grey is another ghostly inmate. For complex political reasons, she reigned as queen for just nine days, during which time she was imprisoned in the Tower of London, where she was executed on 12 February 1554. Another noblewoman, Margaret Pole, Countess of Salisbury, one of the few surviving members of the Plantagenet dynasty after the Wars of the Roses, was also executed in the tower on 27 May 1541. Today, her ghost is also said to haunt the Tower. In addition to these known figures, a number of nameless, formless phantoms have been witnessed at night there, including a bear, and a glowing tubular entity that apparently seized the wife of the keeper of the jewels before letting go of her and disappearing.

GLAMIS CASTLE

The Grey Lady is a ghost who reputedly haunts Glamis Castle in Scotland. Within the castle is a small chapel that seats around 45 people. According to tradition, one seat in the chapel is always reserved for the Grey Lady, their resident ghost. When the chapel is used by the Bowes-Lyon family, who own the castle, the seat always remains empty for the ghost and no one is allowed to sit in it.

Legend has it that the Grey Lady is the ghost of Janet Douglas, Lady Glamis, who died in 1537. Because of a family feud between the Douglas family and King James V of Scotland, the king falsely accused Janet of witchcraft. This was a serious charge at the time, punishable by death, and she was imprisoned in a dungeon of Edinburgh Castle, along with her husband, who managed to escape but was later put to death.

BURNED AT THE STAKE

Although King James wanted Janet convicted as a witch, he found it difficult to find any witnesses who would speak against her. She had a widespread reputation as a morally upright person, and was respected by all those who knew her. Faced with this difficulty, the king set about torturing her family members and servants, trying to extract a confession from them that she was a witch. Eventually, Janet was convicted, and was burned at the stake on the esplanade of Edinburgh Castle on 17 July 1537. In a final act of cruelty, the king ordered Janet's young son John to be forced to watch his mother's slow, agonizing death.

Over the centuries, many people have reported seeing the ghost of the Grey Lady in Glamis Castle. These include a former member of the family, Sir David Bowes-Lyon, who told that he had seen a girl gripping the bars of a window in the castle and looking out into the night with a melancholy expression. He tried to address her, but she turned away, as if someone inside the castle had pulled her away from the window.

Playing Cards with the Devil

Glamis Castle has a number of other ghostly residents and was also the setting for William Shakespeare's *Macbeth*. Shakespeare described the killing of King Duncan as taking place in the castle, although in historical fact, he was killed elsewhere. The castle is also famous as the ancestral home of the Bowes-Lyon family, one of whose members, Lady Elizabeth, became the Queen Mother.

One of the most mysterious legends of the castle concerns a secret chamber hidden deep within the castle walls. Legend has it that card games took place here, and that one of the players was the devil himself. Apparently, this came about when the lord of the castle, known as 'Earl Beardie', decided he wanted to play cards. It was a Sunday, and in observance of the Sabbath day, none of his servants would agree to play with him. He got so angry that he shouted out, 'I'd play with the Devil himself if he were here!' Immediately, so the story goes, there was a knock at the door. When the lord told the person to enter, the devil walked in and the two of them sat down to a game of cards. Meanwhile, the servants, peering through the keyhole to take a look at the visitor, were rewarded by sheets of flame coming out of it, which sent them packing. Today, it is said that the lord and the devil continue to play cards in the room, which has since been bricked up.

The Monster of Glamis

Another ghostly legend about the castle concerns the so-called Monster of Glamis. It is believed that a hideously deformed child was born to the family, and that they were so ashamed of it that they kept it out of the public eye. The child grew up in solitary confinement in the castle, in a private suite of rooms which were walled-up after he died. In a variation on this story, each generation of the family bears a vampire child, who is walled-up in the room until it dies of starvation.

The legends may have been inspired by a true story, that of the Scottish Highland clan Ogilvie, who were constantly at war with the Lindsays, another clan from the 15th century. In one battle, the Lindsays walled-up numerous members of the Ogilvies, who were hiding from them in the castle, and left them to die of starvation. Other ghost sightings include that of a small boy servant, who sits patiently on a stone seat inside the Queen Mother's sitting room; a huge armoured knight, who appears at night; and the bent figure of an old woman carrying a heavy bundle in the grounds of the castle. Another guest at the castle told of a loud hammering in the night, but was advised to keep silent on the matter by the owners of the castle.

Ghostly Glamis Castle shrouded in an early evening autumnal mist.

LITTLEDEAN HALL

Littledean is a small village in the Forest of Dean, west Gloucestershire. Overlooking the River Severn sits the mansion known as Littledean Hall. This foreboding property is believed to be the oldest inhabited house in England and there is hardly a room that has not experienced some form of paranormal activity. Over the years many families have resided in this centuries-old mansion, but a number of troubled spirits have refused to leave.

THE LORDS OF DENE

The house gets its name from the Dene family, who were Lords of Dene from c.1080 until 1327. However, deep in the foundations are the remains of a Roman Temple which was possibly built on top of a Celtic Temple. It was not named Littledean Hall until c.1612, when the Pyrke family who owned the property in the early 17th century, redesigned it to the Jacobean style that can be seen today. Although the house is surrounded by beautiful gardens, the building itself could be described as almost sinister, made all the more eerie by the presence of bats. Not ordinary bats, though, rare Greater Horseshoe Bats that have to be left undisturbed for fear of them becoming extinct. The house is dimly lit inside and the walls are lined with dark panelling.

The Dining Room

Several tragic events took place in this room, one of which was during the English Civil War. It is said that Parliamentarians stormed the Hall and a fierce battle broke out between them and the Royalists. The Royalists lost two men – Colonel Congreve and Captain Wigmore – and you can still see the bloodstains on the wooden floor marking the spot where they fell. Then there was the death of two brothers from the Pyrke family who fought over a woman. They sat down to dinner one evening in the Dining Room and began to tell each other about the woman they had fallen in love with, but they soon realized they were talking about the same woman. The pair flew into a rage, drew their weapons and shot each other. Many visitors to the house have reported seeing bloodstains appearing on the walls and the sounds of gunfire or battle in that room.

GHOSTLY MONK

Also seen in the Dining Room is the apparition of a monk, which is not surprising as there is a priest hole just behind the panelling next to the bay window. This hole led to a secret tunnel connected to cellars which were linked to the nearby Grange at Flaxley Abbey. At a time when it was forbidden to practise the Catholic faith, a monk would use this tunnel to come and give the occupants of the Hall holy communion.

THE BLACK BOY

Hanging above the fireplace in the Dining Room is a picture of the property's most famous ghost – the Black Boy. Two black slaves came to live and work in Littledean Hall, a brother and a sister, from the Pyrke sugar plantation in the West Indies. The boy was to become Charles's manservant while his sister was to be a companion for his own son and daughter. In 1744, the slave girl became pregnant and bore a child of mixed race. When the boy realized that Charles must be the father he became so enraged that he strangled his master to death. The ghost of the Black Boy haunts the Dining Room and several other areas inside the house, and a portrait still hangs there to this day, depicting the boy with his master. His troubled spirit is said to remain in Littledean Hall due to his guilt at killing his master, and frustration at upsetting his sister. He appears most frequently in the Dining Room, wearing a silver collar and carrying a lit candle. It is believed the baby was also murdered, though it is not known by whom, and hidden behind a panel in the Rose Bedroom, which would explain the sound of crying which is often heard coming from that room.

THE BLUE BEDROOM

The Blue Bedroom, with its imposing four-poster bed has been closed to guests for 40 years. Too many people have reported feeling uneasy when staying there and some even said they could hear the sound of battle, gunfire and even piercing screams coming from below.

CREAKING FLOORBOARDS

It is not surprising that this ancient house is haunted, considering the history that lays below its foundations. The current owner of the Hall – Mr Macer-Wright – also has several stories to tell about its former inhabitants. Mr Macer-Wright said he was once woken by the door slamming in his bedroom, then a man stormed into his room, walked over to the window and then back to the centre of the room where he stopped. Although the room was in completely darkness it was easy to make out his outline and also hear his rasping breath. The man obviously meant no harm but was troubled in some way and Mr Macer-Wright said he could hear the creak of the floorboards as the apparition left the room.

The Prison in the Woods

Apart from the Hall, Littledean Jail has also been the scene of many paranormal sightings. It stands at the gateway to the Forest of Dean and was designed as a house of correction by Sir George Onesiphorous Paul and a leading architect of his day, William Blackburn. Blackburn died before the jail was completed, but his brother-in-law William Hobson took over the project. The jail is now used as a residence and is occupied by the Jones family who have witnessed first hand former inmates of the jail, including the jailer himself. Luckily for the Jones family the ghosts seem to be friendly, but visitors to the house have witnessed lights flickering, exhibits shaking and even complete blackouts when the power seems to fail for no reason.

BORLEY RECTORY

Borley Rectory has been called 'the most haunted house in England'. A Victorian house built near a village church, it gained the reputation for being haunted after each of the families who lived in it soon moved out, troubled by the strange sights and sounds they heard at night. In 1937, a ghost hunter, Harry Price, launched a major investigation of the property, publishing several newspaper articles and two books on the subject. In 1939, the Rectory burned down.

Borley Rectory was built by a minister, Reverend Henry Dawson Ellis Bull, in 1862. He had the original house, a Georgian mansion, knocked down, and he then rebuilt the Rectory larger to accommodate his family of 14 children. It also appears that there may have been a house there beforehand, dating from the 12th century, which was said to account for the ghosts believed to haunt Bull's house. Legend has it that, in the 13th century, there was a Benedictine monastery in which a scandal took place. One of the monks in the monastery had a secret affair with a nun from a convent not far away. When the affair was discovered, the nun was walled-up in the convent and the monk was put to death. However, it appears that this story lacks historical evidence and may have been made up by Bull's family to make their new house seem more exciting and romantic.

The Ghost of a Nun

The first signs that the house was haunted came when the Bull family moved in. According to local people who worked there, footsteps could be heard in the rooms and corridors when there was no one else in the house. In 1900, a ghost was seen at dusk – a nun walking in the grounds of the house. The rector's daughters followed the nun and tried to make contact, but she disappeared into the undergrowth. After that, the girls often talked to the villagers about the ghost, and seemed convinced that she was haunting the house. Villagers also claimed that on one occasion, a phantom coach and horses driven by two headless horsemen, had been seen driving up to the rectory.

In 1928, the house passed out of the Bull family, and the Reverend Guy Smith moved into the house with his family. Shortly afterwards, his wife

reported that, when cleaning out a cupboard, she found a brown paper package. When she opened it, she found a skull inside. It was later identified as that of a young woman, and the Smiths inferred that this may have had something to do with the reported haunting of the house by the ghost of a nun.

FOOTSTEPS IN THE HALL

The family then began to experience all sorts of unsettling disturbances, which eventually led to

them leaving the house a year later. They reported hearing servant bells, even though the bells were no longer in use, seeing lights going on unexpectedly, and once again, hearing footsteps which could not be explained by the movements of anyone in the family. Mrs Smith also reported seeing the phantom carriage on several occasions, always at night. So troubled were they that they wrote to a national newspaper, *The Daily Mirror*, asking for help. The newspaper put them in touch with the Society for Psychical Research. This

The Most Haunted House in England. Borley Rectory, Suffolk, England. Destroyed by fire in 1939.

society, founded in 1882, conducted scholarly research into the paranormal and was presided over for many years by the famous American thinker William James.

SPIRIT MESSAGES

Unfortunately for the Smiths, their naïve gesture in contacting the newspaper proved unwise. The paper sent a reporter to the house, who wrote a series of sensationalized articles about it, which attracted the attention of nuisance callers. It also engaged Harry Price, a paranormal researcher, to visit the house. Arriving on 12 June, he reported all sorts of new phenomena, including the rapping out of 'spirit messages' that appeared to come from a mirror hung on the wall. In addition, he reported the activity of a poltergeist, throwing objects such as vases and stones around the house. Mrs Smith became suspicious of Harry Price's findings because when he left after his visit, the spirit messages and the poltergeist ceased activity.

New Occupants

Nevertheless, the whole experience was profoundly worrying for the Smiths, not least because of the publicity that the newspaper had generated, so in 1929 they decided to move on. Not surprisingly, no one was very keen to move in once they had gone, but a year later, a new tenant was found: the Reverend Lionel Foyster. Foyster was a first cousin of the Bulls and had a wife, Marianne, and an adopted daughter, Adelaide. It was not long before the Foyster family began to experience the same disturbing phenomena that had frightened the Smiths into leaving. The Reverend reported a number of unexplained incidents: not only did he witness the bell ringing and the poltergeist activity, with stones and bottles being thrown, but on

one occasion, Adelaide was mysteriously locked in her room and the key could not be found. Adelaide also reported being attacked by 'something horrible', and Mrs Foyster was thrown out of her bed one night.

FAILED EXORCISM

As a religious man, Foyster decided to try to exorcize the ghost and began the ceremony, only to find a large stone hurled at him by an unseen person. However, it later transpired that the culprit may have been his wife, Marianne, who, was having an affair with the lodger of the house, Frank Peerless. In order to distract attention from her sexual transgressions, she was said to have made up the stories about the poltergeist. Marianne herself, however, accused her husband of making up some of the tales in collusion with one of the many 'psychic researchers' who were now visiting the house. All this, coupled with the fact that the family were now the subject of press scrutiny and sensationalized reports, caused a decline in the Reverend's health, and in 1937, the family decided to leave Borley Rectory for good.

Paranormal Investigation

After the Foysters left, the rectory was rented by Harry Price, who advertised in *The Times* for 'responsible persons of leisure and intelligence, intrepid, critical, and unbiased' to form a team of investigators who would spend nights in the abandoned house. He assembled a team of 'official observers', mostly young people, many of them students, who spent weekends at the house and reported on what they had heard and seen. However, during this year of study, few poltergeist activities were witnessed. The observers noted unexplained footsteps and movements

of objects around the house, but very little else. Some observers felt a chill in the Blue Room, where the original Reverend's son, Harry Bull, had died, but other than that the events in the house seemed to be quite normal.

TALKING TO THE DEAD

The next development was when the daughter of one of Price's observers, Helen Glanville, reported having made contact with two spirits connected to the house. This happened during a séance in Streatham, South London. Glanville conducted the séance using an ouija board and a 'planchette', or heart-shaped flat piece of wood, that moved around on the board to spell out messages. According to Glanville, the first spirit was a nun. She said that her name was Marie Lairre and that she had been murdered at Borley Rectory. She said that she was French, that she had left her religious order and married Henry Waldegrave, the lord of the 17th-century manor house near the rectory, and that she had been murdered in 1667. Price's response to this news was to claim that this was the nun who had been seen over the years at the rectory, and that she was searching for a proper burial. A Mrs Cecil Baines set to work to try to find historical evidence to back up this story, but despite her careful research, none was unearthed.

THE FINAL FIRE

The second of Helen Glanville's spirits told a more disturbing story. This spirit, who was called 'Sunex Amures' announced that he was about to set fire to the rectory, and that it would go up in smoke that very evening at nine o'clock. The fire would expose the bones of a murdered person within the area. This did not happen. However, a year later, on that same day, a fire did indeed

break out at the rectory, when the new and final owner, a Captain Gregson, accidentally dropped an oil lamp in the hallway. At the time, he was unpacking boxes to move in to the house. The lamp caught fire, and spread quickly around the house, damaging it quite badly. It was said that while the fire was raging, the figure of the nun could be seen in the upstairs window.

LAID TO REST

After the accident the insurance company dealing with the fire determined that Gregson had made a fraudulent claim. Harry Price decided to investigate the cellar of the house before it was knocked down, and claimed that he found two bones of a young woman and a medal of St Ignatius, suggesting that these were the remains of the nun. The bones were taken to the local church, but the parish decided that they were pig bones, and refused to bury them. The bones were then taken to Liston churchyard, where the rector duly buried them in a Christian service, hoping that the spirit of the nun would then be laid to rest for ever.

The Borley Report

In 1956, the Society for Psychical Research published their report, *The Haunting of Borley Rectory*. In it, they concluded that Harry Price's testimony was unreliable, and that many of the phenomena he reported were faked. They attributed the noises of footsteps to rats under the floorboards, and the bells ringing to naturally occurring sound phenomena to do with the odd acoustics of the house. Since then, there have been many books about the haunting, some of them critical of Price and others supportive of his account.

PENDLE HILL

Pendle Hill, situated a few miles outside Skipton in Lancashire, stands majestically at 1,827 feet, towering over several hamlets. It is steeped in history, dating back to the Bronze Age where it was used as a burial ground. By 1612, it was the site of an enormous limestone tower where two families of peasants lived, led by two old ladies named Demdike and Chattox. However, these were no regular peasants, it was believed these families had magic powers and were thought to be in league with the devil himself.

Curses and Rituals

In March 1612, Demdike's granddaughter, Alizon Device, put a curse on a travelling man who had refused to sell her some pins. The unfortunate tinker was rendered paralyzed. Other members of the family were known to make clay effigies of people they did not like. They would then attach human hair and teeth, before slowly crumbling or burning the effigies, causing the intended victim to suffer an agonizing death. Cattle also died without a single mark on their bodies and when they were milked, the milk turned blue. The locals all suspected the families living in the tower but, because they daren't venture on the hill, nothing was done. King James I was on the throne at the time, but his paranoia for religious persecution brought harsh penalties for anyone practising the Catholic faith and with this came an obsession with witchcraft.

WITCHES ON TRIAL

Eventually, a local magistrate by the name of Roger Nowell, decided to take the matter into his own hands hoping to gain favour with the king. He plucked up enough courage to arrest two of the peasants who he feared were witches. They were taken to Lancaster jail to await trial. The remaining members of the family gathered at Malkin tower and started mixing a magic potion in their cauldron in an effort to blow the gates off the jail. However, the magistrate learned of the meeting and within days the remainder of the 'witches' were arrested. After incriminating statements by a few members of the families, they were all found guilty under the terms of the 1604 Witchcraft Act, a crime punishable by death. On 20 August 1612, the prisoners were taken to the moors above the town and hanged.

GHOST WALKS

In the years that followed, many people lost their lives on Pendle Hill, and to this day locals will

not venture up the hill after dark due to the many sinister ghosts and spirits that have been seen, felt and heard there. Despite this, visitors still flock to Pendle Hill and tourists gather to take place in ghost walks and hunts, the experience being even spookier and more intense on Halloween. Apart from haunting the hill, the Pendle witches are also believed to haunt buildings and villages that lie in the shadow of Pendle Hill. Even though it is four hundred years since the famous witch hunts took place, it appears people are as fascinated as ever.

Contacting the Dead

In 2004, the television show *Most Haunted* produced a Halloween special on the story of the Pendle witches and the hauntings that are regularly reported there. The presenters of the show admitted afterwards that it was the most frightening episode they had ever worked on, and nearly all the crew members reported experiencing feelings of strangulation, of being possessed by an evil spirit and of generally feeling unwell. They allegedly made contact with Elizabeth Device, one of the witches who died in jail before she could come to trial. She told the reporters that there were nine other spirits in the room and they all wanted the team to leave them in peace.

UNWELCOME ATTENTION

In 2009, another documentary about Pendle Hill and its witches was brought to a dramatic halt during production. The team were filming in a barn on Pendle Hill, and as the séance to contact the witches begun, three of the production team were struck down by a mysterious illness. Many speculated that the witches did not want to be bothered and so intervened.

The Pendle Witches. Anne Whittle (Mother Chattox) rides to Pendle Hill with her daughter Anne Redferne, on the back of her broomstick.

THE SALEM WITCH TRIALS

Between 1692 and 1693, a series of witch trials were carried out in Massachusetts. Hundreds of people were imprisoned for practising witchcraft, and many of these were convicted and hanged for the felony. The Salem witch trials have since become famous as an example of mass hysteria; in which a moral panic about a non-existent threat results in the unjust persecution of individuals. Among the imagined powers attributed to a so-called 'witch', was the ability to see ghosts.

SPECTRAL EVIDENCE

The witch trials had many bizarre aspects. One of these was the citing of 'spectral evidence' in court. According to this procedure, victims of witchcraft could see the ghost of the witch who was afflicting them and could therefore give evidence against them. The next strange piece of logic was to discuss whether the so-called 'witch' had given permission to the devil to use their shape or form in order to afflict people. It was decided that the devil could not use a person's shape without their permission, therefore, if the victim saw that person when they were being afflicted, it must be that person's fault. This type of evidence, incredible as it may now seem, was ruled as admissible evidence by juror Sir Matthew Hale, an influential English barrister, and the physician and author Thomas Browne, in the witch trials of Bury St Edmunds in 1662.

The Ghost of Giles Corey

One of the men accused of practising sorcery in Massachusetts was Giles Corey, a rich farmer, member of the local church and general pillar of the community. In 1682, his neighbours Ann Putnam, Mercy Lewis and Abigail Williams accused him of witchcraft. Unlike most of the accused, he flatly refused to plead to the charge. He was then tortured to extract a plea, being crushed with stone weights. However he continued to resist, and eventually died from the torture.

After Corey's death, Ann Putnam claimed that the ghost of Giles Corey visited her in the night and asked her 'to write in the Devil's book'. Not content with this story, she added another one a while later. This time, the ghost of a victim apparently murdered by Corey appeared to her, telling her of its grisly death at the hands of the 'dreadful wizard'. Other women joined in

the stories, claiming that Corey's ghost came to them and tried to assault them. Giles' wife Martha, who attended the church at Salem, was also hanged during the witch trials. Later, her son Thomas petitioned for her loss, and was awarded £50 as compensation for the illegal execution of his mother.

PRESSED TO DEATH

After Corey's death, the details of what happened came to light. According to the law at the time, a person refusing to plead in a court of law could not be tried for a crime. However, there were very few who took this action, since the punishment for refusing to plea was severe. It was called 'peine forte et dure' and consisted of stripping the prisoner naked, lying a heavy board on top of him and putting heavy boulders on top of the plank. In addition, the prisoner was given no food, 'save only on the first day, three morsels of the worst bread, and the second day three droughts of standing water, that should be alternately his daily diet till he died, or, till he answered.' Giles Corey was given this punishment, and after two days was asked three times to plead innocent or guilty to witchcraft. He refused to do so, and instead cried out, 'More stones!' More boulders were put on the board, and at one stage the sheriff even stood on top of them. However, Corey continued to resist. According to a witness, Robert Calef, Corey's face became red and his eyes began to bulge; his tongue was also pressed out of his mouth, but the sheriff poked it back in again with his cane. After a final cry of 'More weight!', Corey died.

COREY'S LEGACY

Because Corey had refused to plead, he died in possession of his estate, so it could not be seized by the government. Instead, it passed to his family, in accordance with his will. Playwright Arthur Miller used Corey as a character in *The Crucible*, his famous play about the Salem witch trials, and a number of other writers have also referred to him in their works. Today, Giles Corey remains a symbol of resistance against the evils of mass hysteria, persecution and violence, such as occurred in Germany during World War II. In this sense, the legacy of his 'ghost' is a positive one, often cited as an example of individual bravery and defiance in the face of the 'herd mentality', as well as social and governmental injustice.

Joshua Ward House

Joshua Ward House is a historic building in Salem, Massachusetts, built in 1784 on the site where Sheriff George Corwin, a major player in the Salem witch trials, formerly lived. Sheriff Corwin was responsible for the imprisonment and hanging of many law-abiding citizens accused of witchcraft. As a result of his unjust actions, his family buried him in the cellar of their house to prevent the public disinterring him and desecrating the corpse. Later, he was given a decent burial in a churchyard.

PIERCING STARE

Many tales of ghosts who haunt the site have since been told. According to various reports, an angry old woman can often be seen on the staircase at Halloween, making menacing gestures and fixing onlookers with a piercing stare. However, each time ghost hunters have tried to photograph her, the only image that can be seen on the photograph is a mass of tiny points of light.

RAYNHAM HALL

One of the most famous ghosts of Britain is the Brown Lady, who is said to haunt Raynham Hall, a stately home near Swaffham, on the Norfolk coast. One of the reasons for her fame is that she was photographed for *Country Life* magazine in 1936. The photographers captured a strange, ghostly form coming down the staircase of the house. She appeared as a white mist, in the shape of a woman wearing a veil and a long dress.

The hall, which dates from the 17th century, belongs to the Townsend family, whose most famous member was Charles, Second Viscount Townsend, Secretary of State in the Whig government in the early 18th century. Viscount Townsend was affectionately known as 'Turnip Townsend' because of his interest in farming, which included introducing the growing of turnips in Britain on a large scale. In 1713, Townsend married Dorothy Walpole, sister of the first British prime minister, Robert Walpole. She was his second wife, and rumour had it that she had previously been the mistress of Lord Wharton, a notoriously decadent aristocrat of the period. Accordingly, there was much gossip about her reputation, and fears that she might corrupt the well brought-up young ladies of the area.

Haunting the Staircase

Lady Townsend is said to have died in 1726. After her funeral, a story began to circulate that she had not died and been buried, but that her husband had locked her up in the house, refusing to let her have any contact with the outside world. This is the origin of the 'Brown Lady' legend: Lady Townsend's ghost is said to haunt the oak staircase in the hall, and can often be seen there at twilight. In some versions of the legend, the Brown Lady is a ghost that came to Raynham Hall with Lady Townsend, having moved with her from Houghton Hall, the seat of Robert Walpole.

A JEALOUS HUSBAND?

In the years that followed, there were many sightings of the Brown Lady, and much speculation as to what had occurred to make her haunt the hall. Some believe that it was the result of unfair treatment from her husband, caused by jealousy.

The pair apparently knew each other as children, since Dorothy's father had been made guardian of Charles. When Charles reached the age of 27, he fell in love with the young girl, who was then only 15, and proposed marriage. Dorothy's father, however, objected, thinking that if he agreed, people would assume he was just trying to get his hands on the Townsend's massive fortune. Dorothy, too, may have objected as some claim that she did not share Charles' passion, and in fact found him very unattractive. Whatever the case, Dorothy forgot Charles for a while and became a London socialite. Her behaviour at wild parties

was thought to be quite scandalous, and she was rumoured to be the mistress of the dissolute Lord Wharton. In the meantime, Charles married, but when his wife died in 1713, he proposed to Dorothy, who accepted.

CRUELTY AND STARVATION?

The marriage, however, was not a happy one. Charles took Dorothy's children away from her and left them in the care of his mother. He confined her to her rooms, where she lived out a miserable, lonely life, dying at the age of 40. At the time, her death was announced to have been caused by smallpox, but rumour has it that her jealous husband may have starved her, or pushed her down the oak staircase that the Brown Lady now haunts. Shortly after her death on 29 March 1726, the ghost was seen on the staircase by some servants at the hall. Numerous reports of encountering the ghost persisted, and it has continued to be sighted until the present day.

Empty Eye Sockets

In 1835, the Brown Lady was seen at night by two guests attending a Christmas party at the hall, Colonel Loftus and his friend Hawkins. They described her as looking refined and aristocratic, except for the fact that instead of eyes, she had only eye sockets. She was wearing a muted brown dress, but her face and hands glowed with a strange light.

The ghost was also seen by Captain Frederick Marryat, a British naval officer well known for his sea tales and novels. The story goes that Marryat believed the haunting in the hall to be connected with local smugglers, and went to investigate. The night he stayed, he went up to his room with two friends. On the way, he met a figure with a lantern, who turned and grinned at them with a horrific smile. The Captain apparently shot at

the figure in alarm, but the bullet passed straight through it, hitting the wall behind.

The Telltale Photograph

In 1926, Lady Townsend residing at the hall reported that her son and his friend had seen the Brown Lady. They were able to recognize her from a portrait of Dorothy hanging in one of the rooms of the hall. However, the most important sighting came in 1936, when two photographers, Captain Provand and his assistant Indre Shira, went down to Raynham Hall to take pictures for *Country Life* magazine.

On 19 September at 4pm they set about photographing the main staircase of the hall. As they did, Shira noticed a misty shape going up the stairs. He shouted to the Captain to take a picture, which he did. When the negative was developed, it showed the image of a shadowy shape coming down the stairs. During the process of developing the film, Shira had called in three witnesses, just to make sure that no one thought it was a hoax. The photograph was published in *Country Life* in December 1936, and is still stored in the offices of the magazine.

WHERE IS SHE NOW?

In recent years it has been suggested that Shira could have smeared grease on the lens of the camera. However, experts examining the photograph have declared it to be genuine. For this reason, the photograph is often cited as proof that ghosts exist. The Brown Lady has not been seen at Raynham Hall since the photo was taken. Some ghost hunters believe that she has moved to a road nearby, where she haunts passers by. There are also reports that she haunts Sandringham House, where she appears as a young, happy woman, rather than a careworn little lady dressed in brown.

A ghostly apparition descends the staircase at Raynham Hall, Norfolk, England.

The Salem Witch Trials, 1692. From June to September of 1692, nineteen men and women, all having been convicted of witchcraft, were hanged on Gallows Hill, a barren slope near Salem Village. Then, almost as soon as it had begun, the mass hysteria ended. The witches disappeared, but witchhunting in America did not.

CULLODEN MOOR

Culloden Moor near Inverness, Scotland, was the site of the very last battle to take place on British soil and, not surprisingly, it saw much bloodshed. The Battle of Culloden took place on 16 April 1746 and marked the end of the Jacobite rebellion which sought to restore the Stuart monarchy to the throne. Many soldiers were killed on the moor, and it is their ghosts which can be heard every year, resuming battle, fighting until they reach their inevitable end.

A Bloody Battle

The battle was between the army of Bonnie Prince Charlie, and Government troops, who were aided by Scottish clans led by Prince William Duke of Cumberland. The conditions were harsh as rain had turned the moorland boggy so the fighting lasted barely 40 minutes. The battle started with an exchange of artillery but without the guidance of Bonnie Prince Charlie – who took no part in the battle – his troops floundered and the slaughter began. Those who were not killed by bullets were cut down in their tracks with bayonets and swords. There was no mercy for the wounded soldiers lying on the ground, they were killed where they lay and any who had managed to flee the fighting were hunted down and killed. On that day, the entire Jacobite army had been killed, even innocent women and children were not spared in the massacre of Culloden. Bonnie Prince Charlie managed to escape by seeking refuge in the Highlands of Scotland before returning to his birthplace in Rome. He never returned to Scotland while he was alive, but in death his ghost has haunted his favourite Scottish

hotel – the Salutation Hotel – in Perth. In 1745, Bonnie Prince Charlie had used the hotel as his headquarters and his ghost has regularly been seen in the bedroom that he used.

HAUNTED MOOR

The killing on the day of the Battle of Culloden was merciless and brutal and it is not surprising, therefore, that the moor is haunted by the many men who lost their lives there. Ghostly soldiers appear on the anniversary of the battle, and the sounds of marching, cries of battle, and the clash of steel can be heard. It is also said that the birds do not sing on that day over the moor and that the local heather never grows on the graves of the Jacobite soldiers.

HARBINGER OF DOOM

The day before the battle, 15 April 1746, a large, black bird was spotted on Culloden Moor by Jacobite Commander, Lord George Murray. He noted the mysterious way it appeared through the fog and the ominous manner in which it traversed

the moor. After the battle, the bird came to be known as the Great Scree of Culloden Moor, and because of its first appearance on the eve of the conflict, it was soon associated with bad luck. In the years that followed many began to see the bird as an embodiment of Lord George Murray's spirit, and to this day many walkers have seen the ghostly bird flying over the moor and wondered if its curse remains.

A GHOSTLY WHISPER

One ghost in particular appears time and time again, that of a tall Highlander who walks the moors. If approached he has been heard to say the word 'defeated' in a whisper. One woman claims that she lifted a tartan cloth lying over one of the graves to find the apparition of a dead Highlander lying beneath it. There are also many drinking wells on the battle site and one in particular, St Mary's Well, is said to be haunted by the troubled ghosts of the dead Highlanders and their cries have been heard emanating from the water.

Paranormal Investigators

An investigative team named Scottish Paranormal, who carry out ghost hunting on a voluntary basis, have reported finding unexplained paranormal activity on and around the area of Culloden Moor. There is a great fluctuation in temperature at the spot where many of the soldiers were killed and investigators are unable to give an explanation why this area should be so much colder. From numerous witness accounts it appears as if the dreadful battle of 1746 is being played over and over again – seemingly a trauma that these troubled soldiers cannot forget.

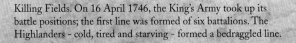

Killing Fields. On 16 April 1746, the King's Army took up its battle positions; the first line was formed of six battalions. The Highlanders - cold, tired and starving - formed a bedraggled line.

ST LOUIS CEMETERY ONE

The cemeteries of New Orleans have been referred to as Cities of the Dead because of their above ground tombs. In the past, bodies had to be buried in shallow graves — if the caskets were buried deep, the water in the soil would cause the caskets to float. In 1788, a fire killed the majority of the city's population, and soon after, many were affected by a yellow fever epidemic. The number of dead bodies resulted in overcrowded cemeteries, and at St Louis Cemetery One, the staff worked intoxicated so they could deal with the stench of the wet, rotten corpses.

After many failed attempts at keeping the caskets in the graves, St Louis Cemetery One, as well as other burial sites in New Orleans, settled for out-of-ground tombs. The cemeteries were built while New Orleans was under Spanish rule and it was the Spanish who introduced the method of vaults which make up the walls of St Louis Cemeteries One, Two and Three. Nowadays, many of the tombs in St Louis Cemetery One are broken and crumbling, and the surrounding area has many dead ends and twisted paths, enhancing the creepy atmosphere. St Louis Cemetery One is the oldest cemetery in New Orleans and has become famous not just for its dead bodies, but for the ghosts that haunt there.

Voodoo Queen

St Louis Cemetery One is the resting place of Marie Laveau who was the famous Voodoo Queen of New Orleans. In her time, Laveau was well known for freeing African slaves. Rumours say that she lived for a 100 years while maintaining her youth and was so beautiful that people would come from all over just to catch a glimpse of her. Since her death, individuals have been known to practise voodoo rituals at her grave, believing it to be good luck. Tourists and voodoo worshippers would sometimes leave offerings at her grave such as flowers and candles, out of respect. One day, on a tour of the cemetery, a visitor picked up one of the offerings to have a look at. The item suddenly was ripped out of her hands by some unseen force. When another visitor tried to pick up the same object, the same thing happened.

Laveau's ghost has been spotted walking between the cemetery's tombs, and has been described as a small figure, wearing a white gown and turban. There have been reports that her ghost has been heard mumbling a New Orleans voodoo curse at trespassers. In the past, this curse has frightened juveniles away who were vandalizing the tombs. On occasion, her ghostly voice has been so loud that people outside the cemetery walls have heard her. Some visitors have claimed to have seen Laveau's apparition near her tomb and claim to have the proof on camera. Other stories surround the Voodoo Queen, a popular one being that her spirit often takes the form of a cat with red eyes. The legend says that if you see the cat you should run before Laveau says a curse. Despite

The City of the Dead. St Louis Cemetery One, New Orleans, Louisiana.

her frightening presence in death and odd rituals while alive, Laveau had a kind heart so perhaps her ghost is a watcher of the cemetery, ensuring that the dead can rest in peace.

The Monk

Pere Dagobert was a pastor at St Louis Church in 1745. He was very charismatic and had close friends who were active in the revolt against Spain. His friends were shot down by a firing squad and their bodies left to rot out in the rain. Dagobert was horrified that his friends were not allowed the Catholic burials that they deserved so he went to the homes of their families, summoning them to the church. Dagobert had secretly recovered all of the dead bodies and performed a burial service in the church. They were then buried in the torrential rain at St Louis Cemetery One. The dead had pine boxes for coffins, as this was all Dagobert could acquire in secrecy. When Dagobert died, his body was buried under the church's altar. His ghost has been seen many times since, often around midnight mass and dressed more as an archbishop than a priest, wearing a long celebratory Capuchin robe. His ghost has also been spotted walking along the left side of the altar holding a candle, though to the spectator's relief the ghost fades after a few seconds. When he was alive, he was very passionate about his church so it is not surprising that his spirit still lingers there. His impression has also been left in the rain – on some rainy nights witnesses have heard his beautiful voice singing the funeral mass. Some people believe him to be watching over his church, even in the afterlife.

The Cities of the Dead

The Cities of the Dead are known to be dangerous places to travel alone. St Louis Cemetery One houses the graves of many people from all walks of life. The only division between areas of burial is religion. Roman Catholics are buried on one side and Protestants on the other. The high tombs make easy conceals for dangers lurking in the darkness. The cemetery not only houses the ghosts of the Voodoo Queen and Pere Dagobert, but also the wandering ghost Henry. The ghost of Henry has been seen wearing a dark suit, but without the shirt. The story goes that Henry had given a lady, who was supposed to be a friend, his papers for his tomb. However, the lady sold his tomb while he was away, and kept the money for herself. When Henry died, his body was buried in Potter's field. Witnesses have claimed to see him walking about the cemetery looking for his tomb. He has also been seen at burials roaming around, and his voice has been heard on recording equipment stating that he cannot rest. Animal spirits have also been seen running around the graveyard, ghosts of the dead pets of a cemetery keeper in the 1800s. People believe that these animal ghosts prowl about the grounds, eternally looking for their owner.

Spooky Location

The renowned St Louis Cemetery One and the other Cities of the Dead have been popular locations for movies such as *Interview with the Vampire*, *Easy Rider* and *Johnny Handsome*. The old St Louis Cemetery One has become weathered and derelict, a perfect set for a horror movie. However, New Orleans has not lost its charm, and tourists often visit to marvel at the architecture and listen to the many stories associated with the cemetery and the dead who reside there. The cemetery is the oldest surviving cemetery in New Orleans. Its walls made of vaults mean visitors are literally surrounded by the dead, some more awake than others.

THE FLYING DUTCHMAN

The notion of a ship, derelict of human life and manned only by the ghosts of sailors, terrifies those at sea. The story of the *Flying Dutchman* has struck fear into the hearts of sailors for years, not just due to the eerie way it silently bobs along, but because the ghostly light it emits signals imminent doom to those unfortunate enough to see it.

PHANTOMS AT SEA

The *Flying Dutchman* was first mentioned in print in 1795, as part of a travel memoir, *A Voyage to Botany Bay*, by George Barrington. The author wrote:

I had often heard of the superstition of sailors respecting apparitions, but had never given much credit to the report; it seems that some years since a Dutch man-of-war was lost off the Cape of Good Hope, and every soul on board perished; her consort weathered the gale, and arrived soon after at the Cape. Having refitted, and returning to Europe, they were assailed by a violent tempest nearly in the same latitude. In the night watch some of the people saw, or imagined they saw, a vessel standing for them under a press of sail, as though she would run them down: one in particular affirmed it was the ship that had foundered in the former gale, and that it must certainly be her, or the apparition of her; but on its clearing up, the object, a dark thick cloud, disappeared. Nothing could do away with the idea of this phenomenon on the minds of the sailors; and, on their relating the circumstances when they arrived in port, the story spread like wildfire, and the supposed phantom was called the Flying Dutchman…

PORTENT OF DOOM

The story became legendary, and passed into superstition among sailors. It was reported by John Leyden in his memoir *Scenes of Infancy*, published in 1803. He said that when storms were about to break off the coast of Africa, sailors claimed that a spectral ship would appear, known as the *Flying Dutchman*. In this re-telling of the tale, the crew of the ghost ship were thought to be guilty of some dreadful crime; they had all perished and their ghosts were ever condemned to sail the seas afterwards. There are many accounts of how the legend came into being, including the idea that the figure who inspired it was a Dutch captain called Bernard Fokke, who plied his trade in the 17th century. This captain was famous for his speedy journeys between Holland and Java, and it was thought that he must have been helped by dark forces in order to make such quick time.

Murder on Board

Another variation of the story is that the captain of the ship, Hendrick Van Der Decken, who himself (not the ship) was known as the Flying Dutchman, ran into a terrible storm on the Cape of Good Hope. However, despite the pleas of his crew, he refused to turn the ship around and head for home. Instead, he sat and drank beer, singing obscene songs and smoking his pipe, while the waves threatened to overturn the vessel. Terrified of losing their lives, the crew mutinied, whereupon the drunken captain shot the leader and threw his body overboard. Legend has it that a voice then boomed down from heaven, telling the captain that he was condemned to sail the seas forever more, never to reach port or know a moment's peace, in atonement for the murder. Over a long period, details were added to the story, such as the idea that the ghost crew would hand out letters to the living, addressed to loved ones who had died long ago. If a sailor accepted these letters, it would bring him bad luck. In addition, if the ghost ship was seen in bad weather, which it most often was, through mist and water, this would mean that the sailors might soon be shipwrecked and drowned.

Fata Morgana

The legend continued to survive into the 19th and 20th century. One memorable sighting was reported by the tutor of the young King George V,

'The Flying Dutchman's on the reef. We've used up all of our time. And the surf's too steep to climb'. Wood engraving, late 19th century.

who accompanied him on a long voyage at sea. He wrote that when they were off the coast of Australia, a phantom ship emitting a ghostly red light was seen in the night, but that it suddenly disappeared. The following morning, the unfortunate sailor who had seen the phantom ship fell off the rigging and was killed. The German Admiral Karl Doenitz reported during World War II that U-boat crews had logged sightings of the *Flying Dutchman* off the Cape Peninsula. This proved to be a bad omen for the crews, many of whom later met their deaths. Various quasi-scientific explanations have been advanced as to what the *Flying Dutchman* might be. Some argue that it is a type of mirage known as a Fata Morgana, which is very rare. This kind of mirage distorts distant objects greatly, and usually occurs at sea. It happens when rays of light pass through different thermal bands and are refracted by the process. From a distance, this refraction of light may create distorted images, which could resemble a bulky shadow on the horizon, such as a ship. The process often takes place in cold waters, because ice gives off refracted light, and for this reason, sightings of the *Flying Dutchman* have mostly been reported in the North Sea.

Another strange optical illusion occurs when rays of light bend and refract in such a way that a ship or other object appears to hover just above the sea. This phenomenon is called 'looming' and may, some argue, account for sightings of a ship that seems to float above the water in a ghostly fashion.

Tales of the *Flying Dutchman* have inspired many poets, writers, and filmmakers over the centuries, from the 18th-century poet Samuel Taylor Coleridge, who based his *Rime of the Ancient Mariner* on aspects of the legend, to the contemporary film series *Pirates of the Caribbean*, in which a ghost ship called the *Flying Dutchman* appears.

The Lady Lovibond

Another strange legend about a ghost ship concerns the *Lady Lovibond*, which was commissioned by Simon Reed in 1748 for a cruise to Portugal to celebrate his marriage. He brought his new bride Annette on the trip, regardless of the superstition at the time that it was bad luck to bring a woman on board a ship. In this instance, it was particularly unfortunate, since the First Mate, John Rivers, was in love with Annette. An altercation ensued which ended with Rivers driving the ship into Goodwin Sands, a notorious ten-mile sandbank in the English Channel. All aboard the ship died when it ran aground and the incident was forgotten. On the same day, 13 February, 50 years later, fishermen spotted a wreck on the sands. A team of investigators were sent out but nothing was found. Over the years that followed, the ship was seen again, emitting a ghostly green glow.

The Eliza Battle

The *Eliza Battle* was a luxury paddle steamer launched in 1852, which plied the Mississippi while the rich and famous were entertained on board. However, in 1858, a fire broke out on board and it sank, killing 26 people out of 100. Today, during spring floods and under a full moon, the wreck is said to rise up out of the water, covered in flames and with music blaring, and paddle down the river. Those who see it take it to be a bad omen, and thus, at that time of year and under the full moon, many avoid looking at the spot where the wreck still lies.

WHALEY HOUSE

Whaley House is considered to be the most haunted property in San Diego and has been officially listed by the United States Department of Commerce as an authentic haunted house. The plot that Whaley House occupies was once the site of San Diego's public gallows, and so has been the scene of numerous executions. Many troubled spirits lurk on this land, and when the Whaley family moved in, their luck began to change.

The house is situated in the old part of San Diego and was designed by a man called Thomas Whaley. It was built in 1857 and was the first of its kind in San Diego. The property was considered a mansion at the time, and the house was used for much more than just a family residence. It contained a granary, the County Court House – which was a room leased by the city in 1869 – the town's first theatre, Whaley's own general store, a ballroom, a billiard room, a school and even a polling station.

The Family

Thomas Whaley was married to a pretty, petite woman by the name of Anna Eloise and the couple moved into Whaley House on 22 August 1857, immediately after its completion. They had three children, Francis, Thomas Jr and Anna Amelia, but Thomas Jr suffered from scarlet fever when he was just 18 months old and died in the house. After his death and a serious fire in the wood store, the family decided to leave Whaley House and move to San Francisco. The Whaleys had three more children, George, Violet and

Corinne and, aware they needed more space, Thomas headed back to San Diego in the summer of 1868 to get Whaley House ready for his family to move back. Anna and the children followed in December, just in time for Christmas. For a short time, life was good for the Whaleys, but soon they were struck by tragedy. Violet, who married in January 1882, was so ashamed when her marriage broke down just a couple of years later, she took her own life by shooting herself in the heart with her father's gun on 19 August 1885. In total, six immediate members of the Whaley family died in the house – Thomas Jr, Violet, Anna Eloise, Francis, George and Corinne, and it appears none of their spirits can rest.

The First of Many Sightings

It was in the 1960s that the house was officially designated as a 'Haunted House' and is now a popular attraction to visitors hoping to catch a glimpse of a ghost. The first ever mention of a ghost being seen at Whaley House is that

of 'Yankee Jim', whose real name was James Robinson. He was convicted of grand larceny in 1852 and hanged on the gallows on the site where the house now stands. Although Thomas Whaley had attended the hanging, he was not deterred by the lands' history and decided he would still like to build his house in that location. However, soon after the family moved in they could hear heavy footsteps moving around the house and found that windows kept flying open even though no one had released the latches. The exact position in the house where Yankee Jim was hanged is an archway between the parlour and the music room, and several visitors have reported feeling a tightening around the throat when standing there.

Whaley House Museum, San Diego, California, USA
as it is today.

THE HEAD OF THE HOUSE

Many visitors have reported seeing Thomas Whaley himself. Whaley loved nothing more than to enjoy a Cuban cigar and the smell of the smoke is sometimes so overpowering that visitors have had to leave the room. His booming laughter is heard all around the house, but he is most often encountered standing at the top of the stairs or in his old bedroom wearing a long coat and a top hat.

GHOSTLY MUSIC

Anna Eloise was a keen pianist with a beautiful voice, and the sound of music can often be heard coming from the family's music room. Once, the keys on the piano were seen moving, but there was no one playing. Her ghost has been sighted all over the house and there is usually a distinct smell of perfume as the spectre floats by. She has also been spotted picking flowers in the garden, which was not an unusual sight when she was alive as she loved to have a vase of fresh flowers in the house at all times.

ANT POISON

One of the most playful ghosts to be seen around Whaley House is Marion, Thomas and Anna's red-haired granddaughter who died at the age of 11 after she inexplicably consumed a large amount of ant poison. She is usually seen by children and appears in such a life-like form that they do not realize that she is a ghost until she mysteriously vanishes from the room. She particularly seems to love attracting the attention of girls her own age and playfully tugs at their hair and arms, and tickles them until they laugh.

STRANGLED

In addition to the Whaley tragedies, a terrible incident took place on the grounds of their house.

A young girl running down a hill outside the house ran into a clothes line which constricted her throat. The servants brought her into the house, with the clothes line tangled around her, but the unfortunate child died on the kitchen table. Since then a young, blonde girl has been seen running around the garden and the kitchen, and pots and pans have been seen to move about on their own.

PHANTOM PET

Another ghost that is regularly seen by children is that of the Whaley's terrier Dolly Varden. They have reported seeing a spotted dog, similar to a fox terrier, running down the hall and in the dining room with his ears flapping and his tail wagging. His favourite trick is to try and lick the toes of anyone who is wearing open-toed shoes. Little Thomas Jr was the first and youngest to die in the house and his cries can often be heard in his upstairs bedroom. Dolly Varden, who obviously is worried about the crying baby, can often be seen running hurriedly into Thomas Jr's bedroom and out again as if to try and alert someone's attention.

MOVING FURNITURE

Apart from sightings of actual ghosts, curtains in the bedroom windows have been seen to blow as if in the wind, despite the fact that the windows have long since been sealed shut to stop them flying open. Pillows often show indentations as if someone has laid their head there and the rocking chair in one of the upstairs rooms often rocks on its own. Whether you are a believer or a sceptic, this house draws in visitors time and time again. It first opened as a museum in 1960 and although no one can say whether it really is haunted, there is plenty of evidence to suggest it is.

ALCATRAZ ISLAND

Alcatraz Island sits right in the middle of the San Francisco Bay, and if troubled souls come back to haunt the places where they were unhappiest or lost their lives, then this place must rank among the most haunted in the world. Nicknamed the 'Rock' this prison was the home to some of the most dangerous men in the United States - public enemies such as Al Capone, Alvin Karpis and Machine-Gun Kelly to name just a few. Its damp, foggy location and constant winds made this site one of the loneliest prisons ever to be built.

Virtually Inescapable

When the military took over the island in 1859 they erected a fort which was when the island saw its first contingency of prisoners. Its isolation and turbulent waters meant it was virtually impossible to escape from, and two years later Alcatraz started to receive Confederate prisoners. Although the number of prisoners was no greater than 50, they rarely saw daylight, being confined to the dark basement of the guardhouse where the general conditions were grim. The stone floor was their bed and in the cramped conditions they were forced to lay head-to-toe. There was no running water, no heating and no toilets, so disease and infestations were a constant problem. Those that were considered reprobates were punished by being locked up in tiny rooms called 'sweatboxes' or fettered with six-foot chains attached to iron balls to restrict their movement. Bread and water was the best they could expect and many lost their lives during their time of incarceration. By 1902, the population of Alcatraz averaged around 500 men per year, but the buildings were in a desperate need of repair so renovation started in 1904 to try and help improve conditions. The Great Earthquake of 1906 left a large crack across the island but luckily not the prison buildings, so prisoners from the heavily damaged San Francisco jail were temporarily placed in Alcatraz. It never really held high security prisoners until the 1920s when crime became major a problem in San Francisco and the head of the FBI, J. Edgar Hoover, decided he needed an escape-proof prison. Alcatraz was the perfect location and in 1933, the buildings were officially turned over to the Federal Bureau of Prisons.

BATTLE OF ALCATRAZ

A dramatic event that took place on the afternoon of 2 May 1946, was an escape attempt that became known as the Battle of Alcatraz. One inmate, Bernard Coy, managed to pry some bars apart and, after greasing his body, was able to squeeze through the gap and get onto an elevated walkway that was patrolled by armed guards. Coy managed to overpower one of the guards, get the cell keys and some firearms, and release five other inmates. Marines were called in to try and diffuse the situation, but gunfire could be heard on the island for two days. Eventually the marines dropped some grenades into the cell block through holes in the roof. Three of the six inmates were killed during the battle, and two of the three survivors were later executed for killing two guards. The one surviving inmate was given a life sentence for his part. The sounds of this battle have been heard time and time again even after Alcatraz was vacated in 1963.

Haunted Cell Block. Alcatraz Island,
San Francisco, CA, USA.

The Hauntings Begin

Alcatraz was not intended as a place of reform but a place where the criminal would be punished for his crime and, with little in the way of comfort, many of the inmates lost their minds and indeed their souls. Today the spirits of past inmates haunt the shadows of the now empty prison and the fog-enshrouded island. Many visitors have claimed to hear men's voices, shrill screams, whistles, the clanging of metal doors and heavy chains being dragged across the floor. When the prison was occupied, several of the guards reported strange happenings including hearing the sounds of crying and moaning, nauseating smells and something they called 'The Thing', a spectre that floated around with penetrating, glowing eyes. Warden Johnson, who was responsible for meeting new prisoners when they arrived on the island, had no time for ghosts and brushed the stories aside without a second thought. However, he changed his opinion when he heard the sounds of a woman crying while taking a number of guests on a tour of the prison. At the time there were no women on the island and it sounded as if it was coming from inside the walls of the dungeon. When the crying stopped, he explained that he felt an icy cool breeze blowing through the group. Guards also reported hearing the sounds of cannons, guns and screams, often making them believe that somehow a prisoner had escaped, but after checking that all the prisoners were secure it always turned out to be nothing.

MORE SIGHTINGS

The original lighthouse, which was damaged during the 1906 San Francisco earthquake, was eventually torn down, but it has been reported on several occasions that on foggy nights it can be seen looming out of the fog. The flashing green light is clearly visible and it is accompanied by an eerie whistle, vanishing just as quickly as it

appears. Apparitions have also been seen in the warden's house, which has long since been burned to the ground. Several guards say they saw a ghostly man wearing a grey suit, a cap and long sideburns. As they watched in astonishment, the room suddenly turned cold and the stove went out briefly before the spirit vanished.

LAUNDRY ROOM GHOSTS

The laundry room is another place for paranormal activities. Visitors and guards have reported the smell of smoke coming from the deserted room, and when they have investigated, discovered thick black smoke pouring out and causing them to choke. Seconds later the room would be completely free of smoke. No one at the prison can account for this mysterious occurrence, but many have speculated that the smoke is a swarm of angry spirits that remain in the laundry room to torment the guards that work in the prison.

D-BLOCK

The infamous D-Block of Alcatraz is where most of the punishments took place and was comprised of 42 individual cells. Anyone who was sent to D-Block would have no human contact at all and would be served all their meals inside their cell. The only diversion to the complete boredom would be reading, but only material that was approved by the governor. The cells were exceptionally cold as they were facing Golden Gate Bridge from which fierce winds frequently blew. Understandably, this is the area where most of the apparitions have appeared. Unsettled in life, the spirits of these inmates seem to be unable to find a resting place and so remain in their cell for all eternity. They have often been seen sitting in a hunched position or just floating about, as if trying to finally escape.

MYSTERIOUS SOUNDS

The most haunted spot in Alcatraz is an area opposite the visiting room where you can see a large metal door that looks as if it was once welded shut. It was behind this door that a night watchman heard strange metallic sounds like chains clanging together in 1976. When he opened the door and shone his torch down the dark corridor he could hear nothing, but as soon as he locked the door he could hear the sounds again. These sounds can be heard whenever the door is shut, but even if it is propped open just a fraction the noise stops. Much like the laundry room ghosts, no one knows what causes these noises and why they stop when the door is opened. It seems there are troubled spirits lurking in every corner of Alcatraz, deliberately baffling guards to exact revenge for their incarceration.

CELL NUMBER 14D

Several of the guides who takes visitors around Alcatraz have reported feeling a sudden unease as soon as they get close to cell number 14D. It always feels colder than any of the surrounding cells even if the temperature outside is extremely hot. Anyone who has had the courage to walk into the cell experiences a strange tingling sensation to their arms and legs and an overwhelming feeling of despair. This is not surprising as many men perished in cell 14D during the bleak history of Alcatraz. They believe the spirit that haunts this cell is that of an inmate who died in there during the late 1880s. Shortly before his death he could be heard screaming that something with glowing red eyes was inside the cell with him. Even after they opened the cell door and tried to quiet him down, the man kept screaming and shaking uncontrollably. There is no doubt at all that many of the downtrodden souls have never left the confines of Alcatraz Island.

Combermere Abbey, Whitchurch, Shropshire, England, 1891. Lady Combermere's sister Sybell Corbett who was staying at the Abbey at the time took a photograph of the library. The exposure time was one hour, during which time the library was empty. But if you look closely you can see a ghostly image of Lord Combermere sitting in his chair on the left. Nothing unusual, except that Lord Combermere had died the previous week...

MARY CELESTE

The *Mary Celeste* was a large brigantine merchant ship, built in New York by the Joshua Dewis ship builders. On 4 December 1872, the *Mary Celeste* was discovered sailing without any crew. The family of three that had been aboard it, along with the seven crewmen, had vanished into thin air. Theorists have pondered the mystery of the *Mary Celeste* for years, and among many people there is a belief that the ship was doomed and those that stepped aboard, cursed.

The Doomed Captains

The original name of the *Mary Celeste* was *Amazon*, and her first captain was Robert McLellan, the son of one of the ship's owners. Nine days after taking command of the ship, McLellan contracted pneumonia. His health deteriorated rapidly and he died aboard the *Amazon*, in the early stages of her maiden voyage. The next captain, John Nutting Parker, shared the same fate when he took position aboard the ship. Soon after setting sail, the *Amazon* collided with a small fishing boat resulting in him having to return to shore for repairs. While the ship was docked a vicious fire broke out, killing Parker and several of the crew. Later, the ship set sail for the third time and with a new captain at the helm. Disaster struck as the *Amazon* sailed across the Atlantic, colliding again, with a vessel. The impact of the crash was so great that the captain perished, along with a few of his colleagues. It was clear that the ship carried some evil spirit that would take the life of any who dared captain it. After a few years, the *Amazon* was renamed the *Mary Celeste*, a name that the owners thought could mark a new start for the deadly ship.

The Ill-fated Journey

On 5 November 1872, the *Mary Celeste* set sail on its last voyage from New York City, headed for Genoa, Italy. It was captained by 37-year-old Benjamin Spooner Briggs who also had his wife Sarah and two-year-old daughter Sophia on board. Sarah was an experienced passenger as she had accompanied her husband on many occasions. In addition to Briggs and his wife and child, there were seven skilled crew members. The ship itself carried a large cargo of industrial alcohol, valued at $34,000. On the night of 4 December 1872, almost a month after it had set sail, the *Mary Celeste* was spotted by John Johnson, the helmsman of the *Dei Gratia*, another ship sailing nearby. The ship's location was 600 miles off of Portugal and Johnson knew instantly that there was something eerie about the way the *Mary Celeste* seemed to be sailing aimlessly. Johnson was spooked and alerted Captain Morehouse. When Morehouse looked through the spyglass to see what had alarmed his helmsman he was shocked. The *Mary Celeste*, which should have already reached Italy, looked to be deserted. Morehouse could

112

not detect any signs of life on the ship, he noted that the sails were torn and the boat was yawing. He felt anxious so he observed the strange ship for two hours from a distance, but still the *Mary Celeste* seemed deadly quiet.

THE DISCOVERY

Morehouse initially thought that perhaps the boat had been taken over by pirates, a common occurrence at the time. However, once the men climbed aboard the ghost ship they saw no sign of battle or resistance, the crew had simply disappeared. Their belongings remained on board as did most of the cargo. The only papers still aboard was the captain's log book, which had last been written in 10 days prior. Apart from the papers, the only other things missing were the lifeboat, the sextant and marine chronometer. Mostly, everything on the ship was left as it was. However, the clock that was hanging on the wall had stopped working and the iron stove was moved from its original location. The crew's valuables and six months worth of supplies were still aboard, ruling out the possibility of a pirate attack as they would most certainly have plundered the goods. Morehouse could not find any reasoning as to how the crew could vanish suddenly.

RUMOURS

After Morehouse failed to come up with a reasonable theory as to why the ghost ship was left abandoned, drifting in the sea, he decided to take it to shore in hope of making a fortune out of the cargo. However, once ashore, there were whispers that Captain Morehouse had organized the disappearance of the 10 missing crew members. They figured that he would sell the cargo for a large sum of money, a reward for his find. However, this was not the case and a sitting was held at the Vice Admiralty Court to determine what had happened to the abandoned ship. The court did not share the same theories as the local people and praised the crew for their courage. The inquiry into the vacant ship sparked interest from the media and the story of the ghost ship travelled fast. The inquiry showed no sign of piracy, murder, struggle or mutiny. Everyone knew that the story of the vanishing crew was true.

'This case of the *Mary Celeste* is startling, since it appears to be one of those mysteries which no human ingenuity can penetrate sufficiently to account for abandonment of this vessel and the disappearance of her master, family and crew.'

THE CURSE LIVES ON

The strange events and fatal history of the *Mary Celeste* did not discourage owners from buying the ship. James Winchester sold the ship at a huge loss as he was quick to be rid of the damned vessel. New owners soon sold the ship on for unknown reasons. Over the next 13 years the ship had over 17 owners who were all quick to

Ghost Ship. The cabin of the abandoned Mary Celeste as it was found by the boarding party in 1872.

get rid of it. G. C. Parker was the final owner of the *Mary Celeste*. He tried to sink the ship as part of an insurance scam, but was unable to make the ship sink. Parker then tried to burn the ship, but, despite it being made of wood, the ship refused to burn and Parker was arrested for his scam. Before his trial he suddenly died of unknown circumstances, leading many to ponder whether the ship had claimed its final captain as part of its grim tradition.

Theories

Many people had theories about the ghost ship. Dr James Kimble wrote about his theory in *The Secret of the Mary Celeste* and believed that the ship had been hit by a sudden waterspout. His theory was extremely unlikely as waterspouts are not common outside the tropics. Other theories such as insurance fraud, seismic activity, and mutiny surfaced, but could not be proven. Arthur Conan Doyle wrote about the ghost ship in his book *The Captain of the Polestar*. A 1935 film, *The Mystery of the Marie Celeste*, later told the story of the phantom ship. In *The Langoliers*, Stephen King made reference to the *Mary Celeste* and the terror and superstition that surrounds the mysterious story. Despite all of the theories, the one that sticks is that the ship was a doomed vessel that stole the souls of the crew, including Captain Briggs and his family. The theory noted that the ghostly vessel was evil and brought death and destruction to all who stepped aboard. The missing crew was never found but their memory still lives on through the story of the *Mary Celeste*, the world's most famous ghost ship.

Ghost Ships: the Queen Mary

The *Queen Mary* was a transatlantic liner who took her maiden voyage in 1936. She symbolized luxury, wealth, and leisure at the time. In World War II, she was used as a troop ship and later returned to civilian use. In 1967, the *Queen Mary* was retired to Long Beach, where she is now used as a hotel. There have been many ghost sightings on board, and the ship has become the subject of several investigations by paranormal groups in recent times.

One of the people who has reported ghost activity on the ship is Carol Leyden, a long-serving employee. She reported:

I was in the work area, and for some reason I picked up a cup of coffee, went out to the tables, and there was a lady sitting there. I was so fascinated by her dress. She appeared to be in a late afternoon cocktail-type dress from the Forties. She had dark hair, rolled at the sides with no makeup on. She seemed to be very pale, but I never saw her move. I left the table, went up about ten feet, turned around because I wanted to take another look, and there was nothing there.

ECHOES OF THE PAST

Another person on board, marine engineer John Smith, also noted some unusual activity on the ship. On several occasions, he was near the ship's bow, and heard the sound of metal tearing, water rushing and men screaming. Upon investigation, he found there was nothing untoward. However, some time later, he read about an incident on board the ship during the war years, when the ship accidentally collided with a British cruiser named the *Curacoa*, slicing the cruiser in half, and killing over 300 men. John believed that the noise he heard was an echo of the accident.

LIZZIE BORDEN HOUSE

In 1845 in the city of Fall River, Massachusetts, an ordinary house was constructed on an ordinary street. Years later, the property at 92 Second Street became the home of the Borden family, and the scene of two brutal hatchet murders. The famous address is now known as the Lizzie Borden House, and is named after the main suspect in the most shocking crime of its time. Since the grisly events of 4 August 1892, paranormal activity has been reported in the house, and it has become a major tourist attraction as a result.

A Divided House

Andrew and Sarah Borden lived in their home with their two daughters Lizzie and Emma, and their housekeeper Bridget Sullivan. Sarah, Andrew Borden's first wife, soon passed away, leaving her children heartbroken. After their mother's death, Lizzie and Emma grew distant from their father and the family soon became full of conflict and bitterness. Andrew Borden married a kind woman named Abby, which angered his children further. Shortly after their wedding, Andrew decided to distribute his estate among the family members, leaving Emma and Lizzie furious that their father was giving away their inheritance. Tensions grew and the house became divided, with Andrew and Abby living in one part of the house, and the Borden sisters in the other.

Lizzie Borden (1860-1927).

HATCHET MURDERS

On the morning of 4 August 1892, Abby Borden was assisting Sullivan with the household's chores by making up the bed in the guest bedroom. Suddenly, she was struck from behind with a hatchet, not once, but 40 times. The stepmother's mutilated body was left on the floor, bloody and lifeless, and when Andrew returned home, he met the same fate. He was brutally struck with the same weapon 41 times, hacked into with such force that his left eyeball popped out of his head and was sliced clean in half. Just after 11.00 am, Lizzie discovered the dead body of her father and called to Sullivan for help. Moments later, Sullivan found the body of Abby. The police arrived and the investigation began. Despite being related to the victims, Lizzie's dark and sinister demeanour quickly marked her out as the prime suspect. She was known as often being mean and spiteful, leaving those close to her to question her morals and sanity. She was arrested, but with only motive and no tangible evidence found she was acquitted and released to a community which ostracized her and viewed her with suspicion and disdain. The Borden murder mystery has baffled people for years, and though Lizzie was cleared of the murder charges, this playground chant shows the public's feeling on the case:

Lizzie Borden took an axe
And gave her mother forty whacks.
And when she saw what she had done,
She gave her father forty-one.

The Lizzie Borden House at 92 Second Street, Fall River, Massachusetts, USA

Hauntings

Since the bloody Borden murders, the Lizzie Borden House has reportedly been haunted. The paranormal activity has invited psychics and investigators to the house in search of evidence of ghostly goings on. The house, which has since been renovated into a bed and breakfast hotel, has left guests and staff members frightened after witnessing strange occurrences. Some claim to have heard the sound of a woman weeping in one of the guest rooms. Others claim to have seen the ghost of Abby Borden, dressed in Victorian clothing, straightening out the covers on beds – this frightening experience has happened while guests were still in their beds. Some guests have reported hearing conversations in the house when they were the only ones there. Others say they heard the sounds of footsteps running up and down the stairs when they were alone. On some occasions, guests said they even saw shoes moving across the floor. Doors in the house have been known to open and close of their own accord and lights flicker suddenly.

One cynical guest who was staying at the bed and breakfast hotel, claimed that he had seen the outline of a person on his bed. What was spooky is that the room he was staying in was the very same room that Abby Borden was murdered in. Shocked, he went downstairs to find his wife. His wife was alarmed when she saw her husband pale and shaken. He told her what he had seen and they returned to the haunted room together, and found the bed made up perfectly with no sign of the ghost. It seems as though the restless spirits of Andrew and Abby Borden haunt the house that they lived and died in.

PARANORMAL INVESTIGATIONS

The Borden house has been the focal point of many paranormal investigations. Some investigators claim that the house has cold spots that they believe to be caused by spirits. In some photos taken, strange shapes and shadows appeared that were not seen by the naked eye. Many orbs have also been captured on camera from different parts of the house. In one photo, a ghostly mist covered the painting above the sofa where Andrew Borden was murdered. Some psychics have said that they believe that Lizzie was subjected to incest by her father and sought revenge on him and his wife. Other people have said that Lizzie had tried previously to poison her family which has since been proven to be true. It came to light that Lizzie had been trying to buy highly poisonous and illegal prussic acid which she would use on her parents. Before their deaths, both Abby and Andrew had been unwell, complaining of vomiting and fever. When psychics have entered Lizzie's room they noted the feeling of pain, anger and oppressiveness. One lady said that she and her friends heard an unknown voice welcoming them into the home. After entering the house they went straight to Lizzie's room where guests reported their bed vibrating during the night and their door slamming. They felt sudden dread, a common feeling of those who entered the chilling room. After a séance, the group of investigators smelt a strong smell of tobacco that suddenly filled the room. They routinely placed cameras and recording equipment in all the rooms. On a tape recorder that was placed in Lizzie's room there was a clear sound of a woman giggling. This startled the investigators as when Andrew and Abby Borden's bodies were found, the maid noted that Lizzie was giggling.

RESURRECTION MARY

Many ghostly stories have emanated from the streets and buildings of Chicago, but perhaps none so compelling as that of Resurrection Mary. She has been sighted many times since her first appearance in the 1930s, but where the earthly body of Mary originated from, no one knows for sure. Her legend remains, however, and to this day motorists keep an eye out for the young girl as she walks down Archer Avenue, disappearing into the distance.

THE LEGEND

The popular theory is that Mary is the ghost of a young girl who was killed whilst hitchhiking down Archer Avenue in the early 1930s. Legend has it that she had spent the evening at the local Oh Henry Ballroom dancing with her boyfriend, but at some time during the evening they had argued and Mary stormed out saying that she was going home. She left the ballroom on that cold winter night wearing just a flimsy white dress and her dancing shoes. She started walking along Archer Avenue towards home, however, she didn't get very far before she was struck by a car. The driver panicked and fled the scene leaving Mary to die on the roadside. She was buried in Resurrection Cemetery wearing the same white dress and shoes. Her restless ghost appears night after night, searching for her boyfriend.

MYSTERIOUS HITCHHIKER

Since that night many drivers have reported seeing a pretty young woman with flowing blonde hair and wearing a white dress walking down Archer Avenue – not as a ghostly apparition but, by all accounts, as a solid human form. Some drivers have stopped to offer her a lift only to find she vanishes into thin air. Other drivers have reported actually hearing a thud and feeling the bump as if they had run over a body as the girl runs out in front of their car, but when they pull over to investigate there is no trace of a body. Some drivers have reported seeing Mary trying to jump onto their car as if to hitch a free ride, presumably back to her resting place at the cemetery.

A few young men have claimed to have met the elusive Mary at the local ballroom, describing the touch of her skin as cold and clammy, and those lucky enough to steal a kiss had the strange feeling of kissing an icy blast of air. After dancing

with Mary for several hours they would offer her a lift home in their car. Mary always accepted and directed the driver north down Archer Avenue. However, as soon as they reached the gates of Resurrection Cemetery, the young woman would open the door of the car and then simply vanish, walking through the gates as if they simply did not exist.

Eye-Witness Accounts

At the nearby police station in Illinois, officers were quite used to drivers coming in visibly shaken and ashen-faced, relating stories of the strange girl they had seen, or knocked into, walking down Archer Avenue. These stories led to the ghost being given the name Resurrection Mary. The stories of sightings continued for decades and the description of the spectre never varied, only those with a better memory or who were brave enough to take a closer look, say she carried a small purse or clutch bag in one hand.

ROMANCING THE GHOST

One young driver in particular, Jerry Palus, had a particularly poignant story to tell. He met Mary in 1939 at the local Liberty Grove dance hall and, having seen her there on several occasions, finally plucked up the courage to ask her to dance. They stayed together for a couple of hours and he gained her confidence sufficiently for her to give him her address. At the end of the evening he offered her a lift home, but instead of going to the address she had given him, she asked if he could drop her off at the Resurrection Cemetery gates. Jerry was not happy leaving this beautiful young woman at such a deserted spot on Archer Avenue and offered to walk her across the street. Mary turned in her seat, faced Jerry and said in a very soft voice, 'This is where I have to get

out … but where I'm going you cannot follow'. Confused, Jerry went to say something but before he could stop her, Mary ran towards the cemetery gates and vanished just before she reached them. Jerry was so worried about what had happened to Mary he visited the address she had given him the following morning. When he explained to the woman who answered the door that he was looking for Mary, the shocked woman replied that it was not possible that he could have been out with her daughter because she had been killed by a car several years previously. Jerry was confused as the pictures above the mantlepiece were definitely those of the young woman he had met the night before. Later, Jerry Palus agreed to several interviews to discuss his experience and claimed that it was so vivid and so shocking that he never really got over it. He died in 1992 and perhaps he has once again been reunited with his beloved Mary.

SCORCHED HANDPRINTS

The strangest story of all took place on the night of 10 August 1976, and this time Mary left some visible evidence behind of her existence. The driver on this night was passing the gates of Resurrection Cemetery at around 10.30 pm when he saw a pretty young woman standing on the far side of the cemetery gates clutching the bars as if she wanted to get out. Aware that he was unable to open the locked gates, he drove a little way down the road to the Justice police station and told them that someone had got themselves locked inside the cemetery. A police officer went to investigate but found no one standing at the gates and the graveyard appeared dark and deserted as usual. He thought perhaps the driver had imagined the whole thing until, on closer inspection, he noticed that two of the iron bars on the cemetery gates had been pulled apart and were bent at

strange angles. Realizing that this would have required incredible strength, he looked closer and found something that chilled him to the bone. Where the bars had been bent there were two definite scorched handprints that had been seared into the metal with incredible heat. This incredible story attracted a lot of unwanted attention from people who wanted to see the evidence for themselves even though cemetery officials denied that anything supernatural had taken place. They tried to remove the handprints with a blowtorch which made them look even worse and ended up removing the two bars completely and placing a temporary wire fence in its place. Instead of quelling the rumours, the act of removing the bars had the opposite effect and caused many people to wonder exactly what the cemetery had to hide.

DISTURBED CEMETERY

Sightings of Mary reached a peak during the 1970s and 1980s during a period when the cemetery was undergoing major renovation work. Many people felt that this caused the spirit of Mary to become upset, worried that her only home would be taken away from her. Although sightings of her are not so common these days, there are plenty of people who visit the area in the hope of catching a glimpse of Resurrection Mary.

No Place Like Home. Resurrection Cemetery, Chicago. The ghost of a young girl known as Resurrection Mary, a victim of a hit and run accident in the 1930s, haunts the streets around the cemetery.

OHIO UNIVERSITY

Ohio University in Athens, USA, was established in 1804. Many students have reported strange happenings in their dormitories and on the site of the creepiest building on campus, The Ridges. Formerly known as Athens Lunatic Asylum, The Ridges was renovated and restored for university use. It is no surprise that eerie presences have been felt in this area, given the numerous corpses of asylum patients buried underground there. Dead students have been seen walking the halls, and spectres of slaves have been seen using the Underground Railroad, eternally escaping slavery via the network of secret passages.

Haunted Halls

Athens has a reputation for being the most haunted city in Ohio, however, most of the ghostly goings on that support this claim occurred at Ohio University, one of the oldest universities in the world. The various dormitories, or halls, have had their fair share of otherworldly activity, the most famous being Wilson Hall. Some people believe that the reason for this is because if you connect all of the cemeteries in the surrounding area it forms a pentagon with Wilson Hall in the centre. There have been many stories about spooky Wilson Hall but the most famous is that of room 428. A female student who had once lived in the room endured a violent death. Since then, students have reported furniture moving on its own, items flying off the walls and smashing around the room. Also footsteps have been heard in the room and one student reported seeing the dead girl's apparition. After all of these accounts, the university decided to close the room indefinitely.

THE PRESENCE OF A POLTERGIEST

Jefferson Hall is the building which houses the most recent of the ghost stories. In fact, there was no paranormal activity reported from the hall until the 1990s. The stories of toilet paper unrolling by an invisible hand, lights frantically turning themselves on and off and doors slamming are a few occurrences believed to be caused by poltergeists. Students have also reported hearing the sound of hundreds of marbles being dropped on the floors above them, even when on the top floor.

One night, some students decided to explore the unused room at the top floor in their dormitory. In the room, they saw a woman dressed as a 1950s school teacher sitting at a dusty old desk. They tried to talk to the woman, but she did not answer. When one student realized she appeared to be floating a few inches off her chair, they fled. Later, they returned to show others, but the door was securely locked. When they managed to get inside, the dusty desk remained but the woman had disappeared.

STUDENT SPIRIT

Another haunted hall is Crawford Hall. The haunting started after Laura Bensek, a young student who had been sitting at her window in 1993, suddenly lost her footing and fell to her death. A year later, residents started experiencing problems. Items would disappear and reappear days later, lights would mysteriously turn themselves on and off and strange noises would often be heard. Things did not improve with time, in fact they worsened. One resident who was lying down for a nap one day, turned off his light and left his door ajar for his roommate. He was woken by a young girl who came into his room and sat next to him. She apologized for waking him and then walked out closing the door behind her. Once he had processed exactly what he had seen he went to his residential assistant (RA) and described the mysterious girl. The RA was alarmed as the student had accurately described Laura Bensek, and the student grew even more disturbed when he learnt he had met her ghost on

At one time there were large public mental institutions serving every part of the state of Ohio. Today, the only one which still stands in anything resembling original condition is the Athens Asylum for the Insane also known as The Ridges.

the anniversary of her death. Other residents have reported seeing Laura's ghost walking down the halls. Some say that when anyone plays the Bob Marley song *Laura*, static interrupts the track.

The Ridges

It is no surprise that The Ridges, a building which once housed the state's psychiatric patients, is a hotspot for unexplained activity. Originally, the hospital was condemned as barbaric and inhumane as many patients suffered the tortures of electric shock and lobotomy. In the 1980s the institution closed and stood dormant for several years before Ohio University renovated it into classrooms, offices and a museum. The building is said to be haunted by the ghost of Margaret Schilling, a hospital patient who disappeared in 1978. Authorities searched for the missing patient but found nothing. A month later, Margaret's dead body was discovered by a maintenance worker on the hospital's top floor. To this day, there is a stain on the floor that is an outline of the dead woman's body. In The Ridges, people have allegedly seen Margaret's ghost wandering around at night.

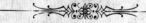

Poltergeist Activity

The amount of paranormal activity reported from Ohio University is phenomenal. A considerable amount of this activity is attributed to poltergeists. Students in the Convocation Centre have reported hearing chairs scraping across the floorboards of vacant rooms. There is a story of a female student who died in her bed. Later, a student who was staying in the same room awoke from her sleep, feeling like she was being held down to the bed by an unseen force. Other residents have reported seeing the ghost of a dead RA who was murdered by her boyfriend, who

believed her to be cheating on him. One closet in the ghostly building throws shelved items on the floor and has a door which refuses to stay shut. The stories have frightened many residents, some who refuse to stay in the building. Bryan Hall is another part of the building believed to be haunted by evil spirits. Students have noted hearing scratching noises on the floorboards and walls, strange whispers and seeing dark orbs. Doors have been seen swinging back and forth frantically and suddenly slamming shut. In Brown House, people have heard the sound of water splashing as though students are playing in a pool. However, there is no pool there anymore. The haunting is rumoured to be by Millie, a resident who drowned at one of her own pool parties. Washington Hall is an area which is home to not one ghost, but an entire female basketball team. Legend has it that a group of young women died in a bus crash as they started to depart from the University. The sounds of basketballs, laughter and chatter is often heard in Washington Hall, the scene of their last ever game.

DISAPPEARING UNDERGROUND

The ghost of Nicodemous, a former slave, allegedly haunts the Alpha Omicron Phi sorority. Nicodemous was shot in the back of the head by a local man who believed that the private house that used to exist on the sorority grounds was hiding slaves. He has been seen disappearing underground, where a secret passage would lead him to freedom. Throughout the years, each sorority group has claimed to experience unusual events. It is evident from the amount of unexplained occurrences that Ohio University is haunted by a number of restless spirits. As a result, it has undergone numerous paranormal investigations and has been voted as one of the scariest places on Earth.

THE WHITE HOUSE

The Presidential residence of the USA, the White House, is said to be home to a number of ghosts. This was first alleged while President Abraham Lincoln was in office. Lincoln believed in ghosts and sometimes sought the advice of a medium to help him with political problems. According to one of his bodyguards, W. H. Crook, Lincoln himself was psychic. Shortly before his assassination in 1865, he told Crook that in a dream he had seen a coffin draped in black in the White House. When he asked what it was doing there, he was told that it was for the president.

Abraham Lincoln's Ghost

After Lincoln's assassination, his ghost was sighted on a number of occasions at the White House. Many reported feeling his presence, but the first to actually see his ghost was Grace Coolidge, wife of the 30th president Calvin Coolidge, who was in office between 1923 and 1929. Grace Coolidge said that she saw the ghost of President Lincoln standing at the window, looking out pensively. Other residents of the White House, including aides and staff, also reported seeing the ghost in the same position.

President Herbert Hoover claimed that he heard 'odd, fantastic' sounds in the building, and staff under President Franklin D. Roosevelt also attested to seeing a ghost. Queen Wilhelmina of the Netherlands once stayed at the White House, in Lincoln's former dressing room, and claimed that one night, she was awoken by a gentle knock on the door. When she got up and opened it, she was amazed to see the ghost of President Lincoln. He took off his tall hat, nodded gravely, and then vanished. In the morning, she told President Roosevelt what had happened, and he admitted that the room was said to be haunted. Another guest, Winston Churchill, also reported seeing the ghost of Abraham Lincoln during his stay.

FOOTSTEPS AND KNOCKS

Subsequent presidents, including Harry S. Truman and John F. Kennedy, also saw Lincoln's ghost frequently. In addition, John's brother Robert also claimed to have seen it. Truman told his guests that the White House was haunted,

reporting that he had heard footsteps and knocks at his bedroom door when he was in bed, but had never got up to investigate them. On one occasion, a secretary saw the ghost sitting on a bed and pulling on his boots. Over time, she got over her fright and continued to see the ghost while she was working there.

To date, the hauntings at the White House have not been adequately explained. It may be that there is just one ghost, or several ghosts – or

that the people who have seen it have simply imagined it. Yet, as has been pointed out, it seems unlikely that so many people, most of them in high office, or employed there, would lie about such an unusual event. Whatever the case, to this day, the spirit of Abraham Lincoln lives on at the White House, and continues to remind residents and visitors of his untimely death all those years ago.

The ghost of Abraham Lincoln haunts the White House. Five days before his death in 1865, Lincoln saw his own coffin draped in black in a dream.

UNION CEMETERY

Union Cemetery in Easton, Connecticut, USA, is said to be one of the most haunted places in the state. Over the years paranormal investigators have been drawn there, gathering photographic and video evidence. Many tourists also visit with the hope of spotting the famous White Lady who has been seen by several witnesses. Visitors have also claimed to have seen a spectre that has been named Red Eyes, in the shadows. Unusual mists have suddenly appeared out of nowhere, some of which have been captured on camera.

White Lady

The White Lady, who has been seen several times around the cemetery, is believed to be the spirit of a woman who was murdered in the 1940s. The rumour goes that she had murdered her husband and is now bound to the cemetery as a ghost. Others believe her to be the spirit of a woman who died during childbirth and has since roamed the cemetery looking for her child. However, only assumptions can be made regarding her identity. The spirit has been described as having long black hair and wearing a white gown. Visitors have claimed to see her ghostly apparition floating among the headstones with a gloomy look upon her face. Drivers along route 59 have said that they have been alarmed to find the White Lady in the middle of the road. Some have stopped, believing her at first to have been hit by a car or stranded, when she suddenly vanishes before their

eyes. One driver claimed to witness the woman standing in the road while he was driving. After braking, he noticed the figure of a man with a straw hat sitting beside him in his passenger seat. The spirit of the White Lady has been spotted countless times over the last 50 years and is the most active spirit in the notorious cemetery.

I saw a woman standing farther up the road so I tapped on the brakes. As I tapped on the brakes, I felt something touch me. I looked over and there was a gentleman sitting in my seat. The woman raised her hand up...and what I remember the most was her hand got very large. As soon as that happened, I looked back over and the image I had seen next to me disappeared.

PARANORMAL INVESTIGATION

Paranormal Investigators Ed and Lorraine Warren led an investigation in Union Cemetery. The

couple are famous for being the investigators of the Amityville hauntings (see page 133-8) and are known for investigating some of America's most haunted places. While Ed was setting up his tripod, he saw a glow in front of him. He rushed to his van to get his camera and moments later the glow took the form of the White Lady. Ed thought that the image of the woman looked around 30 years old. However, the ghost was not alone. Ed claimed to have witnessed black shadowy figures surrounding her looking as though they were trying to consume her. This claim supports other stories from people who said that they witnessed the White Lady arguing with some dark figures. Suddenly, the White Lady started walking towards Ed but after a few paces she vanished. After the investigation ended, Ed and Lorraine rushed home and gathered a party to watch the first viewing of the White Lady caught on camera. To their delight, the apparition was clear on the tape, just as Ed had remembered. This evidence is incontrovertible proof to any doubters who may believe the ghost sightings to be untrue.

Red Eyes

The White Lady is not the only apparition to make appearances in the cemetery; the mystical apparition known as 'Red Eyes' has also been seen on various occasions. Witnesses have claimed to see a pair of Red Eyes in the graveyard, usually at night. Visitors have reported feeling that they were being watched constantly, seeing the glow of the Red Eyes in their peripheral vision. They noted that they would also hear footfalls behind them as they walked which sounded as though some unseen force was following them. Unlike the ghost of the White Lady, the Red Eyes gave the people who had witnessed them the feeling of unease and dread. They have been thought of as

belonging to the shadows which have been seen trying to engulf the White Lady's spirit. Others have believed it to be the spectre of Earle Kellog who in 1935, was set on fire and killed. The story goes that the redness that the witnesses saw was the burnt eyes of Kellog whose spirit now haunts the cemetery. A group of young boys, who were trying to capture electronic voice phenomena, reported that the spirit of a man who had been killed by a drunk driver had provided his name as proof that he was the ghost known as Red Eyes.

EVIL INFLUENCE

It has been thought that Union Cemetery has an evil aura that invites disaster. Locally, a young boy had claimed to be possessed by a demon, a man had used dynamite to try and kill himself and a woman had tried to stab her husband at night for no apparent reason. These terrible events all happened within a close radius of the cemetery. Two young girls were also killed in a car crash just next to the cemetery. Because of the cemetery's history and tragedies that have occurred near its walls, it is no surprise that people believe its evil aura to have some influence on the strange events. These days, many people visit the cemetery in hope of catching some unexplained phenomenon. Police have had to patrol the grounds as teenagers have been known to stake out there. One night a police officer saw a teenager wandering the cemetery. While following the trespasser, small stones kept landing at the officer's feet as though the juvenile was trying to provoke him. He caught sight of a teenager going behind a bush but when he followed, there was no one there. Similar happenings occur regularly in the cemetery which has gained a reputation for its ghosts and ghouls. It seems that Union Cemetery, which is over 400 years old, has a few ghosts with unfinished business.

Spiritual Presence, Newby Church, Ripon, Yorkshire, England. The Rev. K. F. Lord
took this photograph of the church altar in the early 1960s. The ghost only appeared
after the film was developed

HIGHGATE CEMETERY

Highgate Cemetery in North London first opened in 1839 and has been a popular haunt for ghostly figures over the centuries. It was a fashionable area of London to live and also became a chic place to be buried. The Victorians liked to celebrate death and because of this the cemetery offered a wealth of Gothic tombs and buildings which encouraged many visitors. Among the famous who are interred there are Karl Marx, the philosopher and historian, physicist Michael Farady and novelist George Eliot.

Ghostly Sightings

Although it was initially maintained to an exceptionally high standard, by the 1960s Highgate Cemetery had become neglected, and it was during this time that stories of ghostly apparitions started to spread. The misty figure of an old woman has been seen regularly walking among the gravestones and many ghostly faces have been seen peering out of the cemetery gates at night as if wishing to escape. In 1963, two teenage girls were walking home from Highgate Village down Swain's Lane past the cemetery's north gate. They were both stopped in their tracks as they saw ghostly bodies emerging from their tombs. Several weeks later a couple were also walking down Swain's Lane when they too were horrified to see something hovering above the cemetery gates bearing the most hideous expression. When several fox carcasses were found in and around the area of the cemetery, completely drained of blood, it was feared that this ghostly apparition, was a vampire.

HYPNOTIC EYES

In the early 1970s the British Psychic and Occult Society of London was informed of the ghostly presence who had been described as a tall, dark figure with red eyes that had the ability to hypnotize anyone who was brave enough to look into them. In fact, the sightings were now so frequent that the Society decided to send their president, David Farrant, to investigate. As soon as the press got wind of the investigation they concocted their own version of events and soon the ghost was being described as a 'blood-sucking vampire', backed up by the story of a young girl who claimed to have been attacked in 1971 by a

tall, dark figure with a deathly white face. Luckily she survived the attack with nothing more than a few scratches to her arms and legs, but the most mysterious aspect of the case was the area where she said her assailant had vanished, an enclosure surrounded by 12-foot walls. If, indeed, it were a ghost then the walls would not have been a problem, but if she had been attacked by a mere mortal they would have had needed a ladder to scale the walls.

SATANIC RITUALS

Stranger still, in 1974 a dog walker returned to his parked car at the gates of Highgate Cemetery to find a newly disinterred body waiting for him on the back seat. He immediately began to panic, wondering who had put it there and why. When he calmed down, he distinctly remembered locking his car, and so checked for signs of forced entry. The doors and windows were securely shut, and his dog frantically sniffed the car, detecting the grim scent of death emanating from inside. It is not clear what happened after this incident, but the conclusion reached by the owner was that local satanists, who were renowned for using the cemetery for their rituals, were somehow involved with this creepy occurrence. Suffice it to say, he never walked his dog around there again.

PARALYZED WITH FEAR

Then the press took a statement from a man who claimed he had been hypnotized by something within the cemetery. He had gone to look round to see if he could find the tomb of a famous

NORTH LONDON CEMETERY, HIGHGATE.

Highgate Cemetery, London. The Lebanon Catacombs, terrace and sepulchres built in the Egyptian architectural style. Wood engraving, 1838.

person but had stayed longer than he intended. The light had started to fade and he was finding it difficult to find his way out. He said he didn't panic but walked calmly around the graveyard trying to find an exit. He suddenly became aware that there was something behind him and he felt the hairs rise on the back of his neck. As he turned he said he was quite literally hypnotized with fear as he saw this tall, dark figure with burning eyes staring directly at him. He is not quite sure how long he stood transfixed to the spot before the ghostly figure vanished, but he later described the experience as paralyzing as he was unable to move any part of his body, almost as if he was being held by some supernatural force.

THE INVESTIGATION INTENSIFIES

Another man, Sean Manchester, was called in to help with the investigation and along with Farrant, decided that the restless spirit of the vampire was that of a medieval nobleman who had been known to practise black magic in Wallachia, a historical region of Romania. Allegedly, his body had been brought to England inside a coffin sometime in the early part of the 18th century. He lived in a house in the West End of London and was buried on the site that later became Highgate Cemetery. Manchester believed his spirit had been roused by modern Satanists carrying out their ritualistic ceremonies in the cemetery. Both Farrant and Manchester decided the best thing to do would be to try and put a stake through the vampire's body, then remove the head and burn it. However, they both disagreed on who would carry out the deadly deed, both wanting the glory but not the repercussions of such an illegal activity. Manchester publicly announced on television that he would have a vampire hunt on Friday 13 March 1970. The situation, however,

got completely out of hand and it wasn't long before amateur vampire hunters swarmed the cemetery, climbing over the walls and gates. This led to several arrests by the police and David Farrant being taken to court being charged with illegal 'vampire hunting'.

EMPTY COFFINS

Despite their best efforts the vampire was never found. Manchester was not happy to give up on the quest, though, and made many return trips to the cemetery over a period of years. At one point he was accompanied by a psychic who claimed she could lead him to where the vampire rested during daylight. She went into a sort of sleepy trance and proceeded to take Manchester to an old catacomb. There was a hole in the roof and Manchester, with the aid of a rope ladder, managed to climb inside the old tomb only to find empty coffins that contained several cloves of garlic – supposedly used to keep vampires at bay.

HEADLESS BODY

A few months later there was a more sinister turn of events when the headless body of a woman was found badly burned not far from the site of the catacomb that Manchester had visited. Farrant again joined Manchester and they increased their vampire-hunting activities. Neither had any success and both, it appears, were later charged with damaging memorials and interfering with body remains – but of course they denied any part in such activities. The spirit of the Highgate vampire has not yet been laid to rest, it appears, as even in recent years people are still reporting a strange figure in and around the area of the cemetery.

THE AMITYVILLE HORROR

The Amityville Horror is one of the most famous cases of a haunting to take place in America. The story of a house that harboured an evil spirit after an entire family was murdered there captured the public imagination, and it is now hard to separate fact from fiction. The book on the subject by Jay Anson, which inspired a series of films, has been the subject of much controversy, but one fact remains - a family did meet a violent end there, and rumours of paranormal activity have circulated the quiet town of Amityville ever since.

Bouts of Violence

The story begins in November 1974, when the DeFeo family were living in a house named 'High Hopes', a beautiful Dutch colonial house at 112 Ocean Avenue in the pleasant suburban neighbourhood of Amityville, Long Island. Head of the family was Ronald DeFeo, a well-to-do businessman who owned a Buick dealership. However, despite the appearance of a happy, successful family, there were tensions and conflicts within it. Ronald DeFeo was a violent man who often fought with his wife Louise. To the children, he was a figure to be feared. The eldest child, Ronald Jnr, nicknamed Butch, was particularly affected by his father's behaviour. Overweight and sullen, he was often bullied at school, and yet his father showed no sympathy.

By the age of 14, Butch had developed a temper of his own and had begun to terrorize his parents.

To placate him, they bought him a speedboat and gave him as much money as he wanted. He began to use drugs and, by the age of 18, turned a gun on his father. The gun turned out not to be loaded, but it was a warning of what was to come.

ANGRY ALTERCATION

Ronald Senior finally lost patience with Butch when, in order to get more money from his father, he pretended to have been robbed at gunpoint. The police were called in, but Butch refused to co-operate with them. After an angry altercation with his father, Butch drove away, but returned later that night.

MURDER SPREE

On Wednesday 14 November, Butch entered the house armed with a rifle. He went upstairs

to his parents' bedroom and fired at his father, killing him as he lay in his bed. He then turned the gun on his mother, also killing her. Next, he went into the bedroom of his two brothers, Mark and John, and fired on them, killing them both. Not content with this, he entered the bedroom of his sisters, Dawn and Allison. Allison woke up, but undeterred by the horrified expression on her face, he shot both girls in the head, and left them dead.

CREATING AN ALIBI

Seemingly unmoved by what he had just done, he took a shower, changed, gathered up his bloody clothes, wrapped them up in a pillowcase and drove to Brooklyn, where he dumped them in the river. He went to work in his father's dealership, and spent the afternoon with his girlfriend, Sherry Klein. That evening he met up with a friend, Bobby Kelske, at a local bar and pretended to phone home. He told Bobby that he was worried that his family were not answering the phone, so they gathered a group of friends and went over to the house. Butch feigned grief when the bodies were discovered and sobbed uncontrollably. But when the police questioned him about his movements on the night, his story began to fall apart.

It did not take the police long to find out what had really happened that fateful night at the house. In the end, Ronald DeFeo Jnr was charged with murder, brought to trial and on Friday 21 November 1975, was found guilty of six counts of murder and sentenced to life imprisonment.

Attempted Exorcism

The murders had been a sensation in the sleepy suburb of Amityville, but they might in time have been forgotten, had the next stage in the story not ensured their legendary status. In December 1975, a new family, George and Kathleen Lutz and their three children, Daniel, Christopher and Melissa, moved into number 112, attracted by the large house, which also had a swimming pool and boathouse in the grounds. When the real estate broker had told the Lutzes about what had happened in the house just a year or so before, they had decided to go ahead with the purchase all the same, because they liked the house so much that its gory past didn't matter to them.

HISTORY REPEATS ITSELF

When the Lutz family moved in, the house was much as it had been when the previous owners, the DeFeos, had lived there. The Lutzes even bought some of the furniture that was already in the house, as part of the deal. To be on the safe side, they decided to have the house blessed by a friend who was a priest, Father Ralph J. Pecoraro. Even though neither of the Lutzes were practising Christians, they felt that it would be wise to banish any evil spirits from the house before they began their lives there. Father Pecoraro (who was named Father Mancuso in Anson's book, to protect his identity) arrived to bless the house just as the Lutzes were unpacking. He went up to the room where two of the family members had been killed, sprinkled some holy water and began a prayer, but as he did, he heard a loud male voice telling him to get out. Afraid of upsetting the Lutzes, he did not tell them what he'd heard, but on reflection, when he got home, decided to telephone them and warn them not to use the room. While he was speaking, the telephone line began to cut out. The priest also reported that later, he developed blisters on his hands that resembled the crucifixion wounds of Jesus Christ.

THE DEMONS COME TO LIFE

As it transpired, the Lutzes did not find the house as agreeable and tranquil as they had hoped. They began to report many mysterious occurrences. George, the father of the family, would wake at night at around three, get up, and check the boathouse. (This was the time the killings took place). He would sometimes hear the front door slam at night, but there was no explanation for this. He also heard music coming from what sounded like a radio, but when he searched for the source of it, could find none. Kathy Lutz began to have intense nightmares, and reported

that she was beaten in her bed. On one occasion she even experienced levitation, when her body inexplicably rose off the bed.

Scratchings and thumpings were also heard at night, and the youngest child Melissa developed a belief that she had an imaginary friend, Jodie, a pig with devilish eyes. George began to imagine that he was possessed by Ronald's evil spirit, and the family began to see green slime oozing under doors and windows. Clouds of flies appeared, as well as sudden smells and chills, and ghostly hooded figures were seen flitting about the house, sometimes throwing or moving objects.

112 Ocean Avenue, Amityville, Long Island, New York, USA, where Ronald DeFeo, his wife, two daughters and two sons were found shot dead.

FLEEING THE DEMONS

George and Kathy Lutz did their best to deal with the situation, trying all manner of remedies, such as blessing the house again, and moving out to her mother's for a while, but nothing seemed to work. After a month or so, the family had had enough. They decided to get out, as the spirit had advised. They left many of their possessions behind and were loathe to go and fetch them. In fact, they never again wanted to see the house that they had loved so much, so terrifying had their short occupancy been.

INSPIRING FICTION

Later, the Lutzes recorded their experiences for Tam Mossman, an editor at the publishing house Prentice Hall. Mossman hired writer Jay Anson to write a book based on the tape recordings, which went on to sell around ten million copies. A number of sequels to this book, by different authors, have since been published, including *The Amityville Horror Part II*; *Amityville: The Final Chapter*; *Amityville: The Evil Escapes*; *Amityville: The Horror Returns*; *Amityville: The Nightmare Continues*; *Murder in Amityville*, *The Amityville Curse* and *The Secret of Amityville*. A series of films based on the books, beginning in 1982, were also made, the first starring James Brolin, Margot Kidder and Rod Steiger, which was a huge box office success.

The extensive novelization and filming of the story has ensured that, over time, the facts of the Amityville Horror, as it has become known, have been somewhat elaborated, to say the least. This has resulted in a good deal of controversy surrounding what actually took place at 112 Ocean Avenue. Critics have pointed out that many of the stories in the books emulate the fictional stories in the popular 1973 film *The Exorcist*. In particular, one noted paranormal investigator, Dr

Stephen Kaplan, made a thorough analysis of the case and voiced his cynicism over the issue.

Land of Demons?

When the Lutzes left the house, New York Channel 5 sent their news team there to film a séance and investigation conducted by Ed and Lorraine Warren, two well-known TV 'demonologists'. Lorraine Warren claims to be a medium and clairvoyant, while Ed Warren specializes in exorcisms. The Warrens reported that while in the house, they sensed an unearthly presence. Lorraine Warren said that she experienced heart palpitations that were due to occult forces. The couple concluded that the house occupied land once used by a Native American tribe to keep sick and insane members in isolation until they died. After their death, the tribe did not bury them, because they believed the land to be 'infested with demons'. The new findings from the Warrens attracted great attention, ensuring that the legend of Amityville continued.

MEDIA SENSATION

By this time, the Amityville Horror had become a sensation. Here was a house right in the heart of suburban America that was apparently well documented to be haunted. The Lutzes, the Warrens and Jay Anson, who had authored the bestselling book on the subject, all appeared regularly on television and radio talk shows discussing the events at Amityville. In 1976, Dr Kaplan weighed in. He alleged that he had attempted to conduct his own investigation at the house and had been thwarted by George Lutz. He announced publicly that the story was a hoax, and that the Lutzes had fabricated the entire thing.

Katch em and Kill em ! Promotional poster for
The Amityville Horror (2005) featuring Ryan
Reynolds as George Lutz.

Horror or Hoax?

In 1979, Ronald DeFeo Jnr's defence lawyer, William Weber, confessed on a radio show, WBAB, to his part in the hoax; he had met with Lutz and the pair concocted the story 'over a few bottles of wine'. Weber's motive had apparently been to get a retrial for DeFeo, citing the influence of the demons on the house as evidence. (Whether such a defence would have stood up in court is another matter.) Lutz's motive, so Dr Kaplan claimed, had been to flee, not from evil spirits, but from a large mortgage on the house that he couldn't afford. Weber and the Lutzes later fell out over the issue, and a lawsuit ensued.

Despite Dr Kaplan's accusations, no one was keen to hear that the sensational Amityville Horror story was actually a hoax. By this time, the house had become a landmark and a tourist attraction on Long Island, and a large number of people, from the writers and filmmakers, to the different parties involved and their lawyers, stood to gain from keeping the legend alive. Thus, Dr Kaplan's claims, which were perhaps also to some degree motivated by a desire for fame and fortune, tended to be ignored, despite the fact that he had made a fairly careful investigation of the house.

Legal Battles Ensue

The new owners of the house at 112 Ocean Avenue, Jim and Barbara Cromarty, tried to put an end, once and for all, to the story of the Amityville Horror. They did not believe that any of the hauntings had ever taken place there, and sued Anson, his publishers, and the Lutzes for making their lives intolerable with the stream of constant visitors drawn there by the alleged hoax.

The Cromartys cited a number of facts in support of their claim. In March 1977, when they first moved in, they pointed out that the door and window fastenings, said in the book to have been broken by demons, were all intact. A supposed 'secret chamber', the so-called Red Room, was just an ordinary storeroom in the basement that the Lutzes knew about before buying the house. In addition, the local Native American tribe of Shinnecock Indians denied the Warrens' claim, that the insane and sick had once been kept on the land and left there to die, causing the house that was built there later to become infested with demons.

THE LEGEND LIVES ON

Today, it seems likely that the Amityville Horror story was entirely fabricated by those involved, many of whom had financial incentives to do so. However, the fact remains that the house at 112 Ocean Avenue was the scene of a horrific event, the murder of an entire family by the eldest son, and as such, the public are fascinated by it. Inevitably, for most people, an air of horror and dread clings to the house. To date, Jim and Barbara Cromarty claim to have been undisturbed by ghosts and demons there – but how many of us would want to live in a house where such a dreadful crime had occurred? Would we not fear that the atmosphere of the place would be tainted for ever more by the six murders that took place there, and perhaps be curious to visit it? Whatever the truth about the Amityville Horror, the story seems to have struck a chord not only with Americans, but with the public around the world, ensuring that the legend will continue to live on for many years to come.

THE ENFIELD POLTERGEIST

Ghosts have a reputation for haunting castles, mansions and grand houses. But they are sometimes said to reside in very ordinary places, as the case of the Enfield Poltergeist attests. The events took place between August 1977 and September 1978, and again in 1980, at a council house in Green Street, Enfield, a run-down area of North London. The family living at the house were Peggy Hodgson, a single parent, and her four children, Margaret, Janet, Johnny and Billy.

One summer evening, Peggy was tidying the house and the children were upstairs playing in the bedroom, supposedly getting ready for bed. Suddenly, a chest of drawers started sliding across the floor towards the door, as if it were being pushed by an invisible ghost. The children became alarmed when they realized that the ghost meant to barricade them into the room. But just as the chest reached the door, their mother came in, disturbed by the noise.

HURLED ACROSS THE ROOM

When she saw that the children, as she thought, had moved the chest, she pushed it back against the wall, only to see that it started to move again, all by itself. Terrified by this strange happening, Peggy and the children ran from the bedroom. But their encounters with the poltergeist had only just begun.

Over the next few months, the 'Enfield Poltergeist', as it became known, turned the lives of the Hodgson family upside down – literally, at times. With no apparent warning, plates, cutlery, pictures, books and toys, would be hurled across the room by the unseen hand. In the end, unable to understand what was going on, and fearing for the lives of herself and her children, Peggy called in the police.

Independent Police Witness

The police came and listened to her story, noting down the events, but without any evidence of the happenings, were unable to assist the family. However, just as they were about to leave, one of the officers, WPC Carolyn Heeps, saw a chair in the living room rise up off the carpet and move slowly and deliberately across the room.

Ms Heeps tried to find a reason for the occurrence. She thought that perhaps the floor was sloping, and placed a marble on it to see if it would roll in the same direction as the chair. She checked the room to see if there was any way the chair could have been wired to an electrical device. But she was unable to find out why the chair had moved, and duly signed an affidavit to confirm her findings.

Press Frenzy

Although the police officers could do nothing to help the family, since no crime had been committed at the house, it was significant that they had seen the chair move, and thus were independent witnesses to the activity of the poltergeist. News of the haunting soon spread and the house was visited by a number of people, including press reporters and mediums. In one case, a photographer reported being hit on the head by a Lego brick. George Fallows, a senior reporter for the *Daily Mirror*, became convinced that a full investigation into the phenomenon was needed. Mrs Hodgson wanted to get rid of the unwelcome visitor in her house, so the Society for Psychical Research, an organization aiming to research paranormal events in a scientific, unbiased way, were called in.

Ripped from the Wall

Two investigators, Guy Lyons Playfair and Maurice Grosse, were sent to find out what was going on. In addition, the society arranged for an independent barrister, Mary Rose Barrington, to check through their evidence. For more than a year, the two investigators visited the house, assembling a great deal of evidence to show that a poltergeist was active there. According to their notes, objects moved about the house of their own accord; strange knocking sounds, seemingly inside the walls, were

Mrs Peggy Hodgson and her family in the living room of their haunted house in Green Street, Enfield, London, 1977

heard; ornaments levitated off shelves; and boxes were hurled across rooms. Finally, one day something happened that left them deeply shocked. As Guy Lyons Playfair later reported,

I really thought someone was drilling a great big hole in the wall of the house. I tore into the bedroom and there was quite a commotion. The whole fireplace had been ripped out. It was one of those old Victorian cast-iron fires that must have weighed at least sixty pounds. It was so heavy even I couldn't pick it up. The children couldn't have possibly ripped it out of the wall. It just wasn't possible. We caught the incident on audio tape, including the fireplace being ripped out of the wall.

Child Levitated

What happened next was even more disturbing. Late one night, when the family were asleep in their rooms, Maurice Grosse was downstairs working on his research. He then heard the sound of one of the daughters, Janet, screaming. He ran to the bottom of the stairs and looked up to see the bedroom door open and the girl being pushed through it, apparently by an unseen hand. Janet was thrown down the stairs and landed at Grosse's feet. He recorded the incident on tape, the first of many strange happenings in which Janet was picked up and apparently thrown about by the poltergeist. In one instance, Janet appeared to float in mid air. Two witnesses swore that they had seen this happen. They were both passers by in the street, who happened to look up at the

The Enfield Poltergeist terrorized the Hodgson family in their bedroom.

house and see the girl hovering above her bed, as if in flight. Today, Janet remembers:

The lady saw me spinning around and banging against the window. I thought I might actually break the window and go through it. A lot of children fantasize about flying, but it wasn't like that. When you're levitated with force and you don't know where you're going to land it's very frightening. I still don't know how it happened.

POSSESSED BY THE DEVIL?

The next phase in the drama was that Janet began to act like a child possessed by the devil. She began to speak in a guttural voice quite unlike her own, and took to swearing violently, insulting those around her. The investigators questioned her when she was in this state, and found out that the possession was by the spirit of a man named Bill. 'Bill' told them that he had suffered a haemorrhage, fallen asleep, and died in a chair in the living room. Recordings were made of these occurrences, but when the BBC went to the house, they found the metal inside the recording machines had been bent and all the recordings were erased.

AN OLD MAN'S RESTLESS GHOST

Janet's habit of speaking in the guttural voice could have been passed off as an excitable young girl playing a prank on the two investigators, were it not for the fact that, when they researched the previous owners of the house, they found that an old man named Bill Wilkins had lived there. Not only this, but he had died of a brain haemorrhage while sitting in his chair in the living room.

True Story or Hoax?

Over the years that followed, controversy arose as to the truth about the Enfield Poltergeist. Doubters pointed to the fact that on several occasions, the children had played pranks on the investigators. For example, in one instance, they hid a tape recorder belonging to one of them, and admitted that they had been planning to tell them that the poltergeist had moved it. However, their trick was uncovered when the tape recording was played back, and the girls were heard planning their prank.

MISCHIEVOUS BEHAVIOUR

Alarmed by the reports that the children might be hoodwinking the investigators, the Society for Psychical Research sent two more investigators, Anita Gregory and John Beloff, to look into what was going on at Enfield. They spent some time with the family in the house and came to the conclusion that the children might indeed be responsible for most of the supposedly paranormal phenomenal. In one instance, they found them bending spoons, which they had intended to tell the investigators was the work of the poltergeist. Janet was also asked by Anita Gregory whether they had faked other happenings in the house. She replied, 'Oh yeah, once or twice just to see if Mr Grosse and Mr Playfair would catch us. And they always did.'

Playfair and Grosse were adamant that a poltergeist was operating in the house and denied the claims that the children's mischievous behaviour could account for all the strange happenings there. Today, Janet admits that she and her sister did occasionally play tricks on the visitors to the house; after all, they were just children, and they became tired, after a while, of all the inspections that took place there. However, she claims that only a very small percentage of the poltergeist activity was faked by them. And she points out that in some instances, such as that of the fireplace being ripped out of the wall, or the chair levitating in front of the police officers, there was no way that two small girls could have effected such happenings, even if they had wanted to.

EXPERT OPINIONS

The investigators remained convinced that a poltergeist was haunting the house. In addition, the barrister, Mary Rose Barrington, found in her independent review for the Society for Psychical Research, that their evidence was compelling. As well as sifting through their findings, Barrington interviewed many of the witnesses, and came to the conclusion that all were telling the truth about what they had seen and heard. In all, there were about 30 witnesses to the events, none of whom had any particular motivation, financial or otherwise, to lie about them.

However, many experts were sceptical about the phenomenon of the Enfield Poltergeist. Professor Chris French, a psychologist, was of the opinion that the girls had faked most of the occurrences. He thought that they were clever, enterprising and full of mischief, and had decided on a campaign of tricking the gullible adults around them. As to the unexplained phenomena that the girls could not have faked, he puts these down to unreliable witnesses who had been influenced by the stories they had heard.

The Enfield Poltergeist Today

In recent years, the Hodgson family have continued to claim that the strange happenings at their home were real. Janet, the child at the centre of the controversy, who was manhandled by the poltergeist on many occasions, is now a grown woman and has this to say: 'I know from my own experience that it was real. It lived off me, off my energy. Call me mad or a prankster if you like. Those events *did* happen. The poltergeist was with me – and I feel in a sense that he always will be.'

Whatever the truth of the matter, the fact that Janet was the source of the activity seems clear. When she moved away from the house for a time, so as to undergo medical examination, the activity ceased. Later, the activity ceased entirely, leaving Mrs Hodgson to live out her old age in the house, in a peaceful and undisturbed manner.

Aftermath of the Haunting

Guy Lyon Playfair wrote a book about the investigation, entitled *This House is Haunted*, in 1980. A film called *Urban Ghost Story*, loosely based on the events at Enfield and starring Jason Connery and James Cosmo, was released in 1998, and in March 2007, Channel 4 broadcast *Interview with a Poltergeist*, once again examining the case. But perhaps the most memorable tribute was in 1992, when on Halloween night, the BBC ran a drama in mock-documentary style, called *Ghostwatch*, telling the story of an adolescent girl in a North London house, who spoke in a guttural voice and appeared to be possessed by a demon. Many viewers believed the drama to be a true-life story and panicked, before being reassured that the show was fiction, not fact.

Section Four

PHANTOMS OF THE IMAGINATION

GHOSTS IN LITERATURE

Ghost stories are one of the most enduringly popular forms of fiction, and continue to be so today. They appear in almost every culture in the world, and are found in folk tales from all nations. As a result, literature is full of ghostly themes concerning troubled spectres and haunted houses.

The Thousand and One Nights

It is not just those in the West that are fascinated by tales of ghosts revisiting the living. They also appear in *The Arabian Nights*, the first edition of which was published in Britain in 1706. These stories went on to influence gothic horror literature of all kinds. The 'framing device' of the stories, known in the original as 'The Thousand and One Nights' is that a king, Shahyrar, finds out that his wife has been unfaithful to him and has her executed. He is so upset that he decides all women are the same, and marries a succession of virgins, all of whom he executes before they can go on to be unfaithful to him. But he then marries a cunning young woman, Scheherezade, who manages to avoid execution by telling him stories. Each night she ends a tale and begins a new one. The king wants to hear the ending to the new story, so he delays her execution. This carries on for a thousand and one nights.

Many of Scheherezade's tales concern ghosts and haunted houses. *Ali the Cairene and the Haunted House in Baghdad* is one of the most famous of these, while *The History of Gherib and his Brother Agib* tells the story of an outcast prince who triumphs over a host of ghouls. The ghouls are described as monsters who eat human flesh, rather like zombies, and this story is thought to be the place where they are first mentioned in the English language.

Shakespeare's Ghosts

Perhaps the most famous ghosts in English literature are those described in the plays of William Shakespeare. These include Banquo, a character in *Macbeth*, who prophesies that Macbeth is about to become king. When Macbeth has him killed, he returns as a ghost, appearing during the middle of a feast. In a dramatic scene, Macbeth is able to see and hear Banquo's ghost, while those around him cannot. Banquo also appears to Macbeth in a vision, showing him that the heirs to the throne will not be Macbeth's, but his own sons. In some interpretations of the play, the vision of Banquo

cannot be seen by anyone, but is an indication that Macbeth is losing his mind.

REALITY OR HALLUCINATION?

Shakespeare also dabbles with the notion of ghosts in other plays, such as *Hamlet* and *A Midsummer Night's Dream*, where we never really know whether the apparitions are real or simply the product of fevered minds. In *Hamlet*, a young prince is visited by his dead father in the form of a ghost. The ghost leads him to a secluded place and tells him that he is the spirit of his dead father. He claims that he was murdered by Hamlet's uncle Claudius, who poured poison in his ear. The ghost asks Hamlet to avenge him. Hamlet arranges for a play, *The Murder of Gonzago*, re-enacting his father's murder, to be staged. He hopes to find out, from Claudius' reaction, whether he was the murderer. When the play is staged and the murder scene performed, Claudius runs out of the room, suggesting to Hamlet that he is guilty, as the ghost foretold.

Hamlet then goes to see his mother, and is spied on by an adviser, Polonius. Thinking Polonius to be his uncle, Hamlet stabs him, only to find he has made a dreadful mistake.

FROM TRAGEDY TO COMEDY

Hamlet's talk of ghosts, together with other strange behaviour, has convinced those around him that he is mad. Meanwhile, Ophelia, Polonius' daughter, loses her mind from grief and is found drowned. The play ends in a general bloodbath, with all the main characters dying.

As well as tragedies, Shakespeare wrote comedies with a supernatural theme. Perhaps the most famous of these is in *A Midsummer Night's Dream*, in which a group of fairies play tricks on four young Athenian lovers and a group of amateur actors in a forest setting. Here, it is the mischievous side of sprites that is celebrated, rather than the more sombre and serious elements of the supernatural that we see in the tragedies.

'Never shake thy gory locks at me'. The guests urge Macbeth to sit and eat but Macbeth says the table is full. When they point to an empty seat, Macbeth is horrified to see Banquo's ghost in his place at the table. *Macbeth Act 3, Scene 4.*

GOTHIC GHOSTS

In the second half of the 18th century an important change took place in the intellectual world, during what is known as the Age of Enlightenment, when scientific and rational beliefs were cherished as the most progressive aspect of humanity. Then, partly as a result of the political upheaval of the French Revolution, and - in Britain - because of the terrible poverty and destruction caused by the Industrial Revolution, there was a reaction against the optimistic values embodied by the Enlightenment.

The belief that science and reason were the key to progress and development was challenged at a fundamental level. Instead of reason, poets, writers and artists began to value feeling, emotion, inspiration and the irrational, arguing that these aspects of our nature lead us to the truth. The primitive aspects of humanity were seen as natural and beautiful, in contrast to the dry, dusty learning of academics and scientists, who the Romantics saw as responsible for the excesses of the Industrial Revolution. In addition, the beauties of nature, rather than the artifice of city life, was praised. As a result of this movement medieval ideas were revived, and artists all over Europe began to look to the past for inspiration. With this the supernatural came back into fashion, including the belief in ghosts.

The Romantic Imagination

Like the modern horror genre, which it gave rise to, the gothic writers and artists loved to create a sense of atmosphere, romance, fear and awe in their work. Often melodramatic in style, the gothic writers rejected the clarity and rationality of the Enlightenment thinkers, and instead, tried to conjure up thrills and adventure, often setting their stories in landscapes that emphasized the failure and decay of human civilization – ancient medieval ruins, wild moors and heaths, dark forests and so on. They were fascinated by what they saw as the deranged gothic spirit of medieval times, and their stories were full of ghosts, haunted houses, hereditary madness, evil curses and centuries-old secrets. They peopled their tales with romantic heroes, evil tyrants, insane maniacs, fallen women and a host of supernatural beings such as ghosts, vampires, werewolves, demons and dragons.

To some extent, it could be argued that the Romantics arose at a period when the worst miseries of medieval life – poverty, brutality, ignorance – were over, at least for the moneyed classes who lived in European cities and towns. Thus, writers and artists could indulge in fanta-

sies of horror, since they themselves were leading relatively comfortable lives, and any real horror was at arm's length. The same could be said today of the way in which we enjoy horror stories about ghosts, vampires and zombies – since we are removed from a world in which brutality, torture, ignorance, superstition and extreme poverty are part of daily life.

The Castle of Otranto

One of the first, if not *the* first, gothic novel to be written in this new vein was *The Castle of Otranto* by Horatio Walpole, the fourth Earl of Orford. Published in 1764, it was promoted as an Italian manuscript discovered in Naples in the 16th century, and the author was given as 'William Marshal'. Initially it had good reviews, but when the press discovered that Walpole had simply pretended to unearth an ancient manuscript, the book was largely dismissed as nonsense. It went on to be enthusiastically received by the public, and influenced many of the major horror writers that followed, including Bram Stoker and Edgar Allan Poe.

The story concerns a Lord Manfred and his family, who live in a castle. Manfred's son Conrad is to be married to a princess, Isabella, but before the wedding day he is crushed to death by a huge helmet that falls on top of him from somewhere unknown. An ancient curse hangs over the occupants of the castle, and Manfred fears for their future. As the story progresses, all kinds of unlikely events take place, just as in a modern-day soap opera: characters turn out to be the sons or daughters of other characters, there are many near deaths, extraordinary adventures and of course, a happy ending.

In later editions of the book, Walpole explained that in the story, he attempted 'to blend the two

kinds of romance, the ancient and the modern. In the former all was imagination and improbability: in the latter, nature is always intended to be, and sometimes has been, copied with success...' At the time, there was an idea that literature should be naturalistic, realistic and true to life, rather than highly imaginative and full of magic.

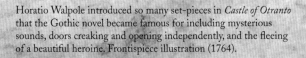

Horatio Walpole introduced so many set-pieces in *Castle of Otranto* that the Gothic novel became famous for including mysterious sounds, doors creaking and opening independently, and the fleeing of a beautiful heroine. Frontispiece illustration (1764).

'Horrid novels'

In the years that followed, the public developed a voracious appetite for the horror and romance elements depicted in the gothic novel. These novels included now-forgotten tales such as *The Necromancer* by Ludwig Flammenberg, published in 1794; *Horrid Mysteries*, by the Marquis de Grosse, published in 1796; *The Mysterious Warning, a German Tale* (1796) by Eliza Parsons; and *The Midnight Bell* (1798) by Francis Lathom.

The fascination with the supernatural, haunted houses, ruined castles, dire curses, ghosts, monsters and all things gothic persisted with the Romantic poets, artists and writers. Notable among them was Mary Shelley, the author of *Frankenstein: Or, The Modern Prometheus*, who created what became the most famous monster of all time. The gothic craze continued into the next century and the Victorian period, when it became more popular than ever, greatly influencing authors such as Edgar Allan Poe, Sheridan le Fanu, Charles Dickens, Oscar Wilde, Henry James, Robert Louis Stevenson, H. P. Lovecraft and M. R. James.

A Christmas Carol

In the Victorian period, classic ghost stories combined romance, horror, folklore and a heavy dose of psychology, a discipline that was emerging at the time and which piqued the public interest greatly. As well as telling tales of ghosts in graveyards, haunted houses and ruined castles, these stories purported to plumb the depths of the mind, attempting to explore the dark, evil forces of human nature, our rela-tion to the sublime, the universe and everything in nature that we cannot understand or explain.

Perhaps the most famous ghost to appear from this epoch is Jacob Marley, the ghost in *A Christmas Carol* by Charles Dickens. This short novel, or novella, appeared in 1843, and told the story of a mean, cruel employer, Ebenezer Scrooge, and his overworked, underpaid clerk, Bob Cratchit. The tale tells how Ebenezer is warned by the ghost of his dead business partner, Jacob Marley, that he should show more kind-

Ebenezer Scrooge face to face with the ghost of Jacob Marley. Charles Dickens insisted that *A Christmas Carol* was illustrated by John Leech. The first edition was printed in colour, which involved very advanced technology for the time, and was very costly.

ness, compassion and charity in his life. Marley tells Scrooge that if he does not change, he will be condemned to a miserable existence in the afterlife. Marley himself is suffering this fate.

VISITED BY THREE GHOSTS

Scrooge is then visited by three ghosts. The Ghost of Christmas Past takes him to visit the scenes of his youth, showing him that he used to be innocent and sweet; the Ghost of Christmas Present shows him around the scene of that Christmas, first of all visiting a marketplace where people are buying lavish food for their Christmas dinner, and then visiting the humble abode of his clerk, Bob Cratchit, and witnessing the dire poverty of the family as the festivities descend. In addition, the ghost takes him to see a miner's cottage and a lighthouse, to emphasize how much help is needed from the rich to improve the lot of the poor. Finally, the Ghost of Christmas Yet to Come shows Scrooge the future, if he does not mend his ways. They visit a grave that nobody has come to tend, and Scrooge realizes that it is his own. As a result, on Christmas Day, Scrooge sends a large turkey to the Cratchit family, and spends the day with his nephew, resolving to heed the ghosts' advice and behave more generously to his fellow human beings in future.

The Canterville Ghost

Oscar Wilde wrote this short novel as a comedy, and it first appeared in 1887. It is set in an English country house, which gives Wilde much scope for comic devices such as clanking chains, prophecies from the grave and bloodstains on the carpet. However, the piece is also a macabre tale, in which the author tells of an American family who go to live at Canterville Chase, ignoring warnings that the house is haunted. The family frequently

bear witness to the fact that the house is haunted by a ghost, Sir Simon, but they are apparently not frightened by it. The ghost is in despair because he cannot frighten the family; they seem impervious to the notion of the dark, gloomy and gothic. Instead, they repair the damage with such products as Tammany Rising Sun Lubricator (to oil the chains) and Pinkerton's Champion Stain Remover (for the bloodstains). In response, the ghost tries to terrify them with apparitions such as the Headless Earl, the Strangled Babe and the Suicide's Skeleton, but nothing phases the family, who play a series of practical jokes on him. Eventually, the daughter of the house, Virginia, takes pity on the ghost and listens to his story, helping him to pass away to the Garden of Death. As in Dickens' *A Christmas Carol*, the story of the ghost is used to express a truth about compassion and forgiveness.

The Turn of the Screw

This novella, published in 1898, by Henry James, is one of the most famous ghost stories in classic English literature. It concerns the story of a young governess who looks after a boy, Miles, and his sister Flora, whose guardian entrusts them entirely to her care at the family estate. The governess sees a man and a woman around the grounds and suspects that they are ghosts. She learns that her predecessor, Miss Jessel, had an affair with another member of staff, Peter Quint, and both had died. She suspects that the children are still in contact with them. Eventually, after trying to protect the children from the ghosts, the boy dies in her arms.

The story is a remarkable and subtle tale in which the malevolence of the ghosts is never obvious or explicit in any way. The author explained that he preferred to write stories that had 'the

strange and the sinister embroidered on the very type of the normal and easy'. Some critics have argued that the story is not a ghost story at all, but an account of the governess's encroaching insanity, told in her own words.

The Modern Ghost Story

Montague Rhodes James, who wrote under the pen name M. R. James, was a ghost story writer and medieval scholar, whose collections appeared in print between 1904 and 1925. He often held parties and told his stories on Christmas Eve, and is remembered today for having set out what he considered the elements of a good ghost story.

Firstly, he felt the story should be set in an interesting place, whether an ancient medieval city, an English country estate, or an austere abbey; secondly, the main character should be a rather dull, scholarly gentleman not given to flights of fancy; and thirdly, an ancient book or antique should be discovered that has special powers to unleash terror, horror, an old curse, a hideous prophecy or some such supernatural element, on the living, as a reminder of the dead. He wrote:

Two ingredients most valuable in the concocting of a ghost story are, to me, the atmosphere and the nicely managed crescendo.... Let us, then, be introduced to the actors in a placid way; let us see them going about their ordinary business, undisturbed by forebodings, pleased with their surroundings; and into this calm environment let the ominous thing put out its head, unobtrusively at first, and then more insistently, until it holds the stage ... Another requisite, in my opinion, is that the ghost should be malevolent or odious: amiable and helpful apparitions are all very well in fairy tales or in local legends, but I have no use for them in

a fictitious ghost story ... Malevolence and terror, the glare of evil faces, "the stony grin of unearthly malice", pursuing forms in darkness, and "long-drawn, distant screams", are all in place, and so is a modicum of blood, shed with deliberation and carefully husbanded.

Ghosts and Horror Fiction

Ghost stories are still a popular literary form, but in the 20th century and the new millennium, they tend to form part of a more generalized type of horror fiction – along with other denizens of the underworld such as vampires, werewolves and zombies. One of the most respected writers in this genre is Stephen King, who often features characters from the horror genre in his work. His 1998 novel *Bag of Bones*, told the story of a ghost haunting a troubled writer. In 2003 King was described as writing 'stylish, mind-bending page-turners that contain profound moral truths – some beautiful, some harrowing – about our inner lives'. However, others have criticized him as 'dumbing down' literary culture and writing 'penny dreadfuls' that compare with the cheap Victorian horror stories of the past. J. K. Rowling includes ghosts in her *Harry Potter* series, however, they are often friendly and such an everyday sight for the pupils of Hogwarts that they are not startled when they appear from thin air. The 2002 novel *The Lovely Bones*, by Alice Sebold, ventured into the afterlife, and imagined her main character, Suzie Salmon, watching her family from her own personal heaven. While Suzie was not depicted as a ghost in the traditional way in fiction, from heaven, her character was still alive and capable of feeling.

GHOSTS IN REALITY TELEVISION

The popularity of such films as *Ghostbusters* gave rise to a number of unusual reality TV shows. In these programmes, a team goes out hunting ghosts in haunted locations, using special equipment for measuring paranormal activity, such as digital cameras, EMF detectors (for measuring changes in electromagnetic fields, said to be caused by ghosts), and thermometers (for measuring cold spots). The shows have, in some cases, attracted controversy, with accusations that the material uncovered is fake, and counter-accusations that all the footage for the shows comes live and direct, without being tampered with. However, shows in this format thrive, as viewers continue to probe the existence of ghosts from the comfort of their living room.

Derek Acorah, one of the psychic mediums of *Most Haunted*.

Most Haunted
2002–2010

One of the first paranormal documentary TV shows was *Most Haunted*, shown on British television in 2002, and thereafter internationally, with several spin-off programmes in different countries. Presented by Yvette Fielding, in its early days it was a high quality production, with stylized shots of the haunted locations, using effects such as dry ice. In addition, the show featured a historian, a parapsychologist and a psychic medium, with the intention of presenting a balanced view of the

phenomena, taking into account both paranormal claims and scientific, rational data. For example, the claims of the medium about people who had formerly lived in the area would be investigated by the historian to see if they could be verified. The locations investigated included Michelham Priory, Owlpen Manor, Bodmin Gaol, Bamburgh Castle, Chambercombe Manor, South Stack Lighthouse, Speke Hall and Berkeley Castle, among many others. The series led to several spin-offs, including *Most Haunted: Midsummer Murders*, an eight-part series in which the investigators tried to solve murder mysteries in English villages such as Nantwich, Castleton, Pluckley, Tutbury and Bakewell.

The mediums included Derek Acorah, David Wells, Gordon Smith, Brian Shepherd and Chris Conway. Derek Acorah, who appeared in many of the shows, was the subject of some controversy after being tricked on television. Told by one of the historians that a couple of non-existent people had lived in the area, he behaved as though possessed by their ghosts. Once these doubts had been raised, the tabloids tried to expose the phenomena investigated on the show, such as bumping and knocking noises, claiming that they were rigged by the TV crew. After these and other complaints, the *Most Haunted* case was taken to the TV regulator Ofcom, which ruled that the show was entertainment, not serious scientific investigation into the paranormal, and therefore was not deceiving viewers. After a long and successful run, the show closed in 2010, to be replaced by a new programme called *Paranormal Investigation: Live*.

Ghost Hunters
2004–

In the US, *Ghost Hunters* was first broadcast in 2004, on the Syfy Channel, featuring two paranor-

mal investigators, Grant Wilson and Jason Hawes. Taking their cue from the eccentric ghost hunters of the film *Ghostbusters*, these friends were both plumbers working for a large American company that clears tree roots from sewers. They had a joint interest in the paranormal, and before their days of TV stardom would go out ghost hunting at night as a hobby, working at their paid job in the day time. They belonged to the Atlantic Paranormal Society, and used a variety of electronic equipment to measure magnetic fields and temperature, as evidence of paranormal activity.

PINPOINTS OF LIGHT

In the show, Wilson and Hawes conduct their tests, try to coax out the ghosts by talking to them, and afterwards discuss their findings with the people who own the house or location where the ghosts are said to reside. Sometimes, they dismiss strange noises, cold spots, unexplained lights, and knocking as due to normal activity, such as vermin running in the walls and roofs, drafty windows and lights from vehicles passing on a road nearby. In most cases, the investigations yield very little; however, in some instances there have been unexplained activities such as shadowy figures, moving objects and pinpoints of light, all of which have been caught on camera and sound recordings.

As well as documentary footage, the programmes also contain an element of soap opera, focusing on the lives of the two presenters, and bringing in other material that happens behind the scenes. In addition, the programme makers have introduced and tested new types of equipment to measure paranormal activity such as a custom-made geophone, which is able to detect vibrations, and a new type of EMF detector which buzzes more and more loudly the closer it gets to an electro-magnetic field. The show has had high

ratings, and has in recent years been syndicated on a number of other channels. The Atlantic Paranormal Society now conducts a number of other activities, such as running an interactive website in which members share their experiences of ghost hunting, presenting shows on radio and organizing lecture tours.

BAD SCIENCE

Over the years, there have been numerous critics of the show, ranging from those who have slammed it as 'terrible television' to those who have questioned its findings, accusing it of peddling bad science and superstition. Even some believers in ghosts and the paranormal have criticized the programme, saying that it does not take the phenomena seriously enough. Investigator Benjamin Radford, editor of the *Skeptical Inquirer*, commented:

> After watching episodes of Ghost Hunters and other similar programs, it quickly becomes clear to anyone with a background in science that the methods used are both illogical and unscientific … I believe that if ghosts exist, they are important and deserve to be taken seriously. Most of the efforts to investigate ghosts so far have been badly flawed and unscientific – and not surprisingly, fruitless.

Ghost Adventures
2008–

The paranormal investigation TV series *Ghost Adventures* was first broadcast in 2008, and starred ghost hunters Zag Bagans, Nick Groff and technician Aaron Goodwin. The series emphasizes the daring side of ghost hunting, with Bagans filling in the macabre history of the sites visited, and conducting interviews with local people who claim to have seen ghosts and other paranormal

phenomena. The sites of paranormal activity are marked out during the day, and then the three heroes are 'locked down' for the night, meaning they stay at the place from nightfall to sunrise, and are left alone by the crew. During the night, they attempt to measure the phenomena, using equipment such as infrared night-vision cameras, and use a variety of tough-talking techniques to try to capture the ghosts. Often, during the shows, the presenters will complain that unseen forces have sabotaged their equipment, causing batteries to drain, and the electro-magnetic measuring equipment to malfunction. In addition, Bagans and Groff claim to have been possessed by spirits at one time or another. Both claim to have been sceptical of such phenomena in the past, Bagans recounting that he did not believe in the paranormal until he encountered the spirit of a woman who had committed suicide in his apartment block. Bagans has been criticized for his macho, aggressive approach to ghost hunting, but has responded by saying, 'I don't want the public perceiving us as the taunting, provocative ghost hunters. We do that only to the bad spirits who we know are attacking the living.'

Ghost Lab
2009

In 2009, the Discovery Channel aired *Ghost Lab*, which followed two brothers, Brad and Barry Klinge, on their ghost hunting adventures. The brothers had founded their own paranormal society, Everyday Paranormal, to investigate unusual occurrences in reputedly haunted locations all over America. Another of Discovery Channel's paranormal programmes is *A Haunting*, which was first aired in 2005 and featured dramatic re-enactments of various well-known paranormal happenings. Also on the show were interviews with individuals who had experienced such events.

GHOSTS IN SUPERNATURAL DRAMA

In addition to the reality shows that investigate paranormal activity, there are numerous television programmes based around ghosts. Supernatural drama is as popular with TV audiences as with avid readers and moviegoers. Whether the ghosts are a threat to society, or helpless spectres seeking the assistance of the living so that they can cross over, shows such as *Eerie Indiana* and the *Ghost Whisperer* appeal to children and adults alike, often gaining a cult following that long outlives the series itself.

Eerie, Indiana
1991–1992

In the early 1990s NBC (then later, FOX) ran a programme about the Teller family, who are new to the neighbourhood of Eerie, Indiana, population 16,661. The Teller's eldest son, Marshall, soon realizes that there are many strange goings-on his new hometown, and with the help of his best friend Simon, decides to investigate. Over the course of the short-lived series, Marshall and Simon become involved in many spooky situations, several of which include encounters with ghosts. The young investigators also explore urban legends, e.g the existence of Bigfoot, and whether Elvis is still alive. *Eerie, Indiana* gained cult status among the young viewers of the 1990s, as it dared to peer beneath the polished surface of suburban conformity and probe the horrors lurking there.

The X-Files
1993–2002

The X-Files, mostly known simply as 'X-Files', follows paranormal investigators Fox Mulder and Dana Scully as they explore the existence of paranormal phenomena and supernatural entities. Ghosts feature frequently in their investigations, in fact, one can be seen walking down a corridor in the opening sequence, as the infamous theme tune plays. The show was a huge success and was praised for its originality, clever script and likeable characters.

Buffy the Vampire Slayer
1997–2003

Sarah Michelle Gellar stars in this programme about a young woman who moves to a small town called Sunnydale in the hopes of escaping her vampire slaying duties. However, she soon discovers that Sunnydale is a hotspot for supernatural activity when she realizes that her high school is built on top of a portal for demons, Hellmouth. As the series progresses Buffy and her friends are faced with battling ghosts, vampires, werewolves, zombies and demons, using a mixture of physical combat and magic.

Charmed
1998–2006

The four Halliwell sisters, Pheobe, Piper, Prue and Paige are the culmination of a long line of good witches, and are known in supernatural circles as The Charmed Ones. Their destiny is to protect innocent lives from demons, warlocks and other supernatural entities such as ghosts.

The Ghost Hunter
2002–2004

The Ghost Hunter, based on the children's books by Ivan Jones, appeared on the BBC in 2002, and was a drama about two children, Roddy and Tessa Oliver, who encounter a ghost in their bedroom. The ghost is William Povey, a poor shoeshine boy from Victorian England. He asks for their help as he is being tracked by a Ghost Hunter, who wants to sap his 'spectral energy', and the children set out on many adventures. Although the series ended in 2004, it was a critical success, and received several awards. *Ghost Trackers*, which currently airs on the HBO TV station in the US, is a reality TV show for children, in which contestants investigate haunted locations and are filmed doing so by hidden cameras. The children who use the technical equipment most effectively, and who are brave and resourceful in their quest, gain the title of 'top tracker'.

Ghost Whisperer
2005–2010

The CBS supernatural drama stars Jennifer Love Hewitt as Melinda Gordon, a young woman who can see and communicate with ghosts. She uses her unusual ability to help ghosts trapped on earth to resolve their issues and cross over to the other side, or into 'the light'. This is not always an easy task, and sometimes she faces many obstacles, but in each episode she resolves to help a ghost finally rest.

Supernatural
2005–

American drama, *Supernatural*, features all kinds of dark characters such as vampires, demons and ghosts. Brothers, Dean and Sam, hunt these creatures from the dark side as they threaten to disrupt their neighbourhood.

Being Human
2008–

British supernatural drama *Being Human* follows the lives of three twenty-something characters sharing a house in Bristol. Mitchell is a vampire, George is a werewolf and Annie is a ghost. Since her death, Annie has haunted the house that Mitchell and George live in. She can sometimes be visible to 'normal' people, depending on her state of mind, but she is always visible to those with a supernatural background.

Jennifer Love Hewitt communicates with earthbound
spirits in the *Ghost Whisperer*, US TV series.

GHOSTS IN FILM

Not surprisingly, ghost tales have often proved fertile territory for filmmakers. Original screenplays, short stories and novels have been adapted for the big screen, with varying degrees of success. Over the decades, movies have dabbled in numerous narratives, and ghosts have been presented to us in different ways and in varying roles.

The Role of the Ghost

Ghosts usually feature as frightening predators doomed to terrorize the living, but they sometimes appear as deceased loved ones, bringing comfort or a message from 'the other side'. Often, a ghost remains on earth because 'unfinished business' needs to be resolved, before the ghost can 'cross over'. The concept that a soul cannot rest until a problem that existed in life is taken care of, is a common theme in ghost movies. Sometimes, the ghost has the ability to interfere with mortals on a psychological level, making a character become hysterical and fear they're losing their mind. This is a clever idea, which relies on subtle scare tactics, and leaves the audience pondering whether the source of the protagonist's issues were all imaginary. In film, ghosts often haunt the place where they died, and react violently to new people inhabiting it. In these cases, the ghost in question is known as a 'poltergeist', and has the ability to move objects or people, alter temperatures and play tricks on the living in order to drive them

out. Ghosts, as a plot device, are not confined to just one genre; they also frequent comedy, fantasy and romance. In these instances, the ghosts are not figures to fear, and sometimes feature as part of a forbidden or doomed romance. Ultimately ghost movies deal with our questions about life after death, and what happens to our soul when we shuffle off this mortal coil.

The Uninvited
1944

The Uninvited, directed by Lewis Allen, is considered to be one of the classic ghost/horror movies in cinema history. The story concerns a brother and sister who buy a country house haunted by two ghosts, one good and one evil. Big on atmosphere and tension, the film has been praised for its nail-biting suspense, and the deft pacing of the narrative.

Dead of Night
1945

This film was formed of a series of short stories grouped together. Each story was directed by a different director, including Alberto Calvalcanti, Charles Crichton, Robert Hamer and Basil Dearden. Starring Michael Redgrave, the film contains a memorably spooky scene involving a ventriloquist's dummy that appears to be possessed by an evil spirit. The film proved to be a tremendous influence on the horror genre, and the idea of the dummy went on to be used in many ghost stories later, both for radio and TV. In 1978, the same idea came up in a film called *Magic*, starring Anthony Hopkins, about a malevolent ventriloquist's dummy who commits a murder.

The Ghost and Mrs Muir
1947

This romantic comedy revolves around a woman who moves into a haunted house and meets the ghost of a handsome sea captain. He recounts the story of his life, which she writes up and publishes, becoming a successful author. At the end of the film, when Mrs Muir dies as an old lady, she is reunited with her handsome beau.

House on Haunted Hill
1959

This ghost story entered 'B' movie territory with this film. It was directed by William Castle and starred Vincent Price. The story follows an eccentric millionaire as he prepares for a 'haunted house party' but what was planned as pleasant entertainment turns into a nightmare, when the guests are trapped inside the house along with a ghostly gallery of rogues and murderers.

The Innocents
1961

This movie was an adaptation of the Henry James novel *The Turn of the Screw* (see page 151-2). Directed by Jack Clayton, it starred Deborah Kerr as Miss Giddens, the governess, and Michael Redgrave as the children's uncle. In the film, the children are represented as freakish and unnerving. later in films, weird children became a common theme in the horror genre, and have remained so to the present.

Carnival of Souls
1962

This low-budget movie was directed by Herk Harvey and starred Candace Hilligoss. The story concerns a car-crash survivor who finds work as a church organist, and begins to see all sorts of spectral figures. In a neat inversion of the traditional ghost story, she realizes that she cannot be seen or heard by the ghouls, and fears that she has joined the ranks of the dead. The film was not a great success at the time of its release, but has since achieved critical plaudits and cult status.

The Haunting
1963

Haunted houses are an ever-popular theme in ghost movies and of these *The Haunting* remains one of the most striking. Directed by Robert Wise, and adapted from Shirley Jackson's 1959 novel *The Haunting of Hill House*, it follows the activities of a group of paranormal investigators as they spend several nights in a haunted house. The film has been praised for the complexity of its characters and its atmospheric shots, and is considered by many to be a classic of the genre. In 1999 a loose remake of the film was released, starring Catherine Zeta Jones, Owen Wilson

HA

starring
VINCENT PR

Produ

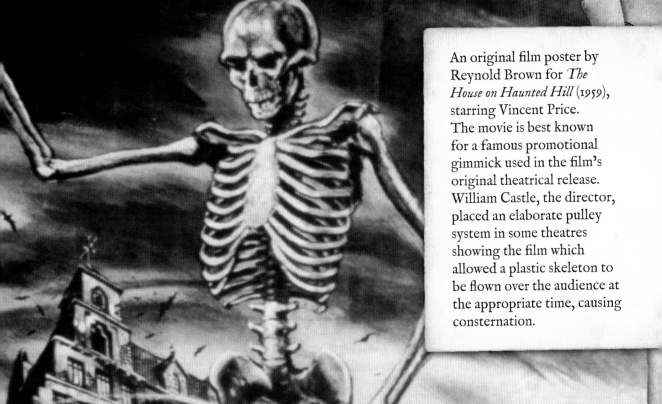

An original film poster by Reynold Brown for *The House on Haunted Hill* (1959), starring Vincent Price. The movie is best known for a famous promotional gimmick used in the film's original theatrical release. William Castle, the director, placed an elaborate pulley system in some theatres showing the film which allowed a plastic skeleton to be flown over the audience at the appropriate time, causing consternation.

HOUSE ON
NTED HILL

E · CAROL OHMART · RICHARD LONG · ALAN MARSHAL

d Directed by WILLIAM CASTLE · Written by ROBB WHITE

and Liam Neeson. The 1963 version was more faithful to the novel it was adapted from, and perhaps this is why the 1999 remake was not as well received. One criticism of the remake was that the movie relied on, and overused, CGI (computer-generated imagery) to deliver its scares, and lacked the subtlety of the original.

The Exorcist
1973

The Exorcist, released in 1973, is perhaps the most memorable film of the 1970s concerning the paranormal. It tells the harrowing tale of demonic possession, based on the true story of Robbie Mannheim, a young boy who was repeatedly exorcised to rid him of what appeared to be an evil spirit. Directed by William Peter Blatty, the film starred Ellen Burstyn, Linda Blair, and Max von Sydow. Often cited as the most terrifying horror film of all time, it was also the most profitable, taking more profits at the box office than any other film of that year. Many urban legends exist concerning the production of *The Exorcist*, as several odd incidents took place during its filming. A priest was called in several times to bless the set, but despite this gesture, there seemed to be a curse on the whole production. Initially there was a mysterious fire which destroyed much of the set and delayed filming. Later, there were two accidents involving harnesses causing injury to the actors. After filming completed, one of the actors, Jack MacGowran, died of influenza. Several other films about demonic possession, violence, and madness followed, including *The Omen* in 1976, which was remade in 2006.

Don't Look Now
1973

Don't Look Now is a film based on a short story by Daphne Du Maurier and was released in 1973. It was directed by Nicolas Roeg, and starred Donald Sutherland and Julie Christie. The story tells of a couple who are mourning the loss of their young daughter who has drowned. They travel to Venice on business, where they meet two elderly sisters, one of whom is a clairvoyant and claims to be in touch with their daughter's spirit. Although there are no actual ghosts in the film, the glimpses of a small person in a red mackintosh, scurrying down misty Venetian alleyways, is unforgettable – as is the terrifying twist at the end of the film.

The Tenant
1976

The Tenant, directed by, and starring, Roman Polanski, tells the unnerving story of a meek young man who takes an apartment vacated by a woman who has committed suicide. The apartment is in a block where the neighbours are not just unfriendly, but positively frightening. Among the strange sights the unfortunate young man witnesses is the occupant in the opposite flat, who appears to be a mummy that unwraps himself every night. The story ends in madness and violence, portrayed by some shocking special effects, such as a bouncing, decapitated head.

Burnt Offerings
1976

Burnt Offerings, based on the novel of the same name by Robert Marasco, offers a new twist on the familiar 'haunted house' theme, in the shape of a house that seems to be trying to kill its inhabitants. This film went on to influence many later films, including *The Shining* and *The Amityville Horror*.

Linda Blair, possessed by demons in *The Exorcist*, 1973.

TOP: Here's Johnny! Shelley Duvall, armed with a butcher's knife, cowers in the bathroom as a fire axe wielded by Jack Nicholson crashes through the door. *The Shining* (1980).

BOTTOM: Jamie Lee Curtis is caught in a killer fog containing zombie-like ghosts seeking revenge for their deaths in *The Fog* (1980).

The Shining
1980

The Shining is one of the most memorable films of the 1980s, and certainly one of the scariest. Directed by Stanley Kubrick and starring Jack Nicholson and Shelley Duval, it was loosely based on the novel of the same name by Stephen King. The plot follows a family of three who move into the off-season Overlook Hotel so the father can work as a caretaker while using the isolation and solitude of the hotel to concentrate on his writing project. The young son, Danny, who possesses psychic abilities and ESP (extrasensory perception) is greeted at the hotel by a chef, who communicates with the boy telepathically. Danny soon begins to see ghosts in the hotel, and has a premonition that something bad will happen there. Soon, the hotel becomes snowbound, and the father descends into madness, influenced by the malevolent spirits in the house. He becomes violent, attempting to kill both his wife and son. The film, which was heavily publicized, had mixed reviews on its release, but today is seen as hugely influential on the horror genre, and popular culture. The film's most memorable line, 'Here's Johnny!', spoken by Jack Nicholson's character as he chops through a door with an axe and sticks his head through the hole, grinning maniacally, has been 'spoofed' numerous times in films, television and music videos. It is claimed the hotel is built on the site of an ancient burial ground, and that is why so many spirits remain there. This concept has been adopted many times (it's central to the plot of *Poltergeist)*, and has come to be considered a narrative staple of the horror genre.

The Changeling
1980

Inspired by events in writer Russell Hunter's life, *The Changeling* centres around the character of Dr John Russell, a composer, who, following the death of his wife and child in a traffic accident, moves into a large and eerie looking Victorian mansion to be alone and reflect on his grief. He soon discovers that he is not, in fact, alone, but sharing the house with the restless ghost of a child who was murdered there. The ghost exhibits poltergeist behaviour; shattering windows, opening and closing doors and making other loud noises before manifesting itself at a séance. Russell begins an investigation that ultimately leads to a powerful local family, the heir of which is a United States Senator.

The Fog
1980

The Fog, directed by John Carpenter, centres around a coastal town which gradually becomes enveloped in a glowing fog, bringing with it the ghosts of mariners who perished in a shipwreck 100 years earlier. The film was remade in 2005 and received mixed reviews.

Poltergeist
1982

Poltergeist, directed by Tobe Hooper and produced by Steven Spielberg, was another hit film of the 1980s, spawning a trilogy, and being nominated for several awards. In the first instalment of the trilogy, Carol Anne, the youngest of the Freeling family, becomes a conduit for supernatural entities who connect to her via the television. The family are then terrorized by a poltergeist who moves objects and bends utensils. The activity eventually escalates to a tree coming alive and

Poltergeist (1982). Legend has it that the series of movies carried a curse, fuelled by the fact that real cadavers were used as props in various scenes of *Poltergeist* and *Poltergeist II*.

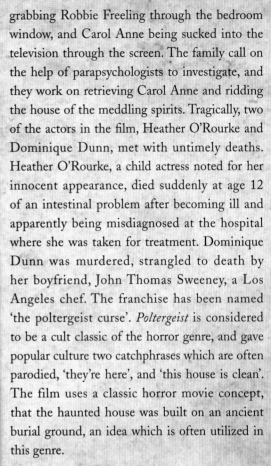

grabbing Robbie Freeling through the bedroom window, and Carol Anne being sucked into the television through the screen. The family call on the help of parapsychologists to investigate, and they work on retrieving Carol Anne and ridding the house of the meddling spirits. Tragically, two of the actors in the film, Heather O'Rourke and Dominique Dunn, met with untimely deaths. Heather O'Rourke, a child actress noted for her innocent appearance, died suddenly at age 12 of an intestinal problem after becoming ill and apparently being misdiagnosed at the hospital where she was taken for treatment. Dominique Dunn was murdered, strangled to death by her boyfriend, John Thomas Sweeney, a Los Angeles chef. The franchise has been named 'the poltergeist curse'. *Poltergeist* is considered to be a cult classic of the horror genre, and gave popular culture two catchphrases which are often parodied, 'they're here', and 'this house is clean'. The film uses a classic horror movie concept, that the haunted house was built on an ancient burial ground, an idea which is often utilized in this genre.

Ghostbusters
1984

Ghostbusters was released in 1984, directed by Ivan Reitman and starring Bill Murray, Dan Aykroyd and Harold Ramis. The fast-paced comedy followed the antics of three eccentric paranormal investigators and featured striking special effects. The film broke box office records and a sequel, *Ghostbusters II*, was made in 1989, along with two animated TV series. *Ghostbusters* is thought to have encouraged the modern craze for ghost hunting, which currently features in several reality TV programmes.

TOP: Who you gonna call? Bill Murray, Dan Ackroyd and Harold Ramis searching for spectres in *Ghostbusters* (1984).

BOTTOM: 'Let's turn on the juice and see what shakes loose!' Michael Keaton as the freelance 'bio-exorcist' ghost in *Beetlejuice* (1988). The original script was a horror film, and featured Beetlejuice as a winged, reptilian demon. Subsequent script rewrites turned the film into a comedy and turned Beetlejuice's character into the ghost of a wise cracking con-artist rather than a demon.

Beetlejuice
1988

Beetlejuice was directed by Tim Burton and starred Michael Keaton, Geena Davis and Alec Baldwin. It is known as a 'black comedy', due to its morbid yet funny plot. Barbara (Davis) and Adam Maitland (Baldwin) are a young married couple who decide to decorate their New England home instead of going on holiday. On their way to pick up some supplies, their car crashes through a covered bridge and plummets into a river. In the next scene, the couple walk into their home, soaking wet, and start to discover that things are not quite right. They realize they don't have a reflection, and they can't recall how they made their way home. When they notice a book entitled *Handbook for the Recently Deceased*, they come to the conclusion that they did not survive the crash. Struggling with the news, Adam tries to leave the house, only to be transported to another dimension, a world covered in sand and filled with large worm-like predators. As the Maitland's start to come to terms with being dead and bound to their home, the obnoxious Deetz family from New York move in. The family consists of Charles, his second wife Delia, and his daughter, Lydia. Charles is craving the quiet life of suburbia, whereas Delia, an aspiring sculptor, is immediately bored and tears the house apart, removing any trace of the Maitland's style. Barbara and Adam contact Juno, their case worker in the afterlife, who advises them on how they can get rid of the Deetzes using various ghostly tricks. Meanwhile, it becomes apparent that Lydia Deetz, a teenager with gothic tendencies, can see the Maitlands and they become friends. When the Maitland's tricks, including a scene where they possess the Deetzes, fails and the family refuse to be scared away, they turn to a 'bio-exorcist' named Beetlejuice, against the advice of Juno. To make him appear they must say his name three times. Once they meet him they realize that contacting him was a mistake, and that rather than helping them, he seems intent on marrying Lydia, so he can come back to life. The Deetzes and Maitlands eventually combine efforts to send Beetlejuice back to the afterlife, and the two families decide to co-exist in the same house. At the end of the film we see a transformed Lydia, achieving at school with the help of the Maitlands, and a much happier Charles and Delia. Unlike other ghost stories, these ghosts remain in their home, and do not 'cross over' at the end of the story. *Beetlejuice* delves into the afterlife and imagines what it might look like. It explores the concept that there is an organized process that awaits the recently deceased, e.g an office we go to and a case worker that is assigned to us. The character of Beetlejuice also represents the idea that in death, as in life, there are tricksters about who want to take advantage of people. The ghosts of Barbara and Adam also have the ability to possess objects or people, and can even levitate them, a characteristic not shared by many other fictional ghosts.

Ghost
1990

Directed by Jerry Zucker, *Ghost* is a romantic fantasy drama starring Patrick Swayze, Demi Moore, and Whoopi Goldberg. It focuses on the relationship between Sam Wheat (Swayze) and Molly Jensen (Moore). Sam is a banker who confronts his colleague and best friend about a major financial discrepancy at work. Later, Sam and Molly are attacked, and Sam dies as a result, his ghost rising out of his corpse and overlooking the scene. Sam's ghost sees Molly crying over his body and he realizes that not only is she unable to see or feel his presence, but that her life is in danger from the man who killed him. Oda Mae

Brown (Goldberg) then comes into the picture. She is a con-artist who claims to be a medium, however, when Sam contacts her, she – reluctantly at first – accepts that she can hear the dead, after all. It is then up to Sam to convince Oda Mae that she should contact Molly in order to save her life. *Ghost* explores what happens to our spirit, or soul, when our physical body expires. In Sam's case, the second he dies a 'living' copy of him is visible. A beautiful spotlight then pours down onto him, but as he stares at Molly weeping over his dead body, the light disappears and he is left at the scene. In the case of two other characters, the villians of the piece, when they die, tiny black demons appear from nowhere and drag them away, to hell, presumably. Later, when Sam's mission is over, the bright light appears once again, and Molly can now see and hear him. He then disappears into the light.

Heart and Souls
1993

Directed by Ron Underwood, *Heart and Souls* is a fantasy/comedy about the ghosts of four deceased people who, through a twist of fate, are reliant on Robert Downey JR's character, Thomas Reilly, to help resolve their unfinished business on earth so that they can 'cross over'. Following in the tradition of *A Christmas Carol*, by Charles Dickens, the plot sees ghosts acting as mentors in the life of the central character, in order to convey a wider lesson for humanity, which, in this case, is something akin to 'Seize the Day'.

Haunted
1995

This British film returned to the foundations of the ghost movie genre using key elements such as an old haunted house, a sceptical investigator, misty lakes, shadows and fog, rattling door knobs and unexplained noises in the night. As the story unfolds, the investigator David Ash, played by Aidan Quinn, uncovers that all is not what it seems in the house, and realizes that there is something otherworldly about its residents. The film received mixed reviews, with some enjoying the return to a traditional ghost story, and others claiming the classic formula was dated and lacking in suspense.

Casper
1995

In the 1930s a hugely popular comic-strip and animated cartoon was aired. called *Casper the Friendly Ghost*. The series inspired the 1995 feature-length movie *Casper* starring Bill Pullman as James Harvey, and Christina Ricci as Kat Harvey, his teenage daughter. The Harvey's move into an old mansion at the request of the spoilt Carrigan Crittenden (Cathy Moriaty), who has inherited the property along with the three obnoxious ghosts that haunt it. James Harvey is a therapist who believes he can talk to the dead, and Carrigan wants him to convince the ghosts to cross over to the other side. As they move in they discover a fourth ghost, Casper, to their initial horror, and come to learn that the three ghosts are his uncles. Over the course of the film Kat struggles to make mortal friends, and Casper wishes he were alive again. As a ghost, Casper cannot recall all of his short life, and sometimes it takes certain objects to jog memories. He discovers his old sled which reminds him of how he died, and in turn he remembers that his father was an inventor, a clue which leads to Kat and Casper coming across his invention, the Lazarus Machine, which can bring the dead back to life. When James gets killed after a boozy night out with the uncles, he returns to the mansion in ghost form, and Casper

makes the hard decision to let James drink the potion and come back to life, and so Casper remains a ghost.

Casper and his uncles were brought to life using CGI at a time when this technology was cutting edge. Mostly the actors were working with thin air, and the ghosts were added in later. The film was aimed at a young audience and critics questioned how appropriate it was to run moments of comedy and slapstick alongside issues of death and the afterlife. Despite this juxtaposition, the film was a success at the box office.

The Frighteners
1996

The Frighteners is the brainchild of splatter stick pioneer Peter Jackson, who co-wrote and directed it. It stars Michael J. Fox as Frank Bannister, an architect who develops psychic abilities following his wife's tragic and untimely death. He turns his new-found skills to his advantage by setting up a ghost hunting business, paying ghostly associates a fee to haunt buildings so that he can be called in to save the day. Things are going relatively well until the ghost of a serial killer returns from hell and begins killing off his client base, whereby Frank takes it upon himself to track down the killer and send him back to where he came from. The film received mixed reviews, and was not a financial success at the US box office. This is widely attributed to competition from the film *Independence Day*, which was in theatres at the same time, but Peter Jackson blamed Universal's marketing campaign, particularly a poster that 'didn't tell you anything about the film'.

'Can you keep the secret?' Child psychologist Malcolm Crowe (Bruce Willis) takes on the task of curing a young boy (Haley Joel Osmont) who 'sees dead people'. *The Sixth Sense* (1999).

The Sixth Sense
1999

Bruce Willis and Haley Joel Osment starred in this 1999 hit film written and directed by M. Night Shyamalan. The movie recounts the tale of a disturbed young boy, Cole Sears, who can see and communicate with the dead, and his psychologist, who is experiencing the breakdown of his marriage. *The Sixth Sense* is packed with suspense, and often the ghosts we see through Cole's eyes are frightening and creepy, still marked by the method in which they died. The film culminates in a twist ending which shocked audiences and left film buffs endlessly re-watching it in search of clues. *The Sixth Sense* was nominated for six Academy Awards including Best Picture and, although it did not win these prestigious awards, it became an instant classic of the genre.

The Blair Witch Project
1999

The most original film of the 1990s was released in 1999 and presented as a piece of documentary filmmaking. Co-directed by Eduardo Sanchez and Daniel Myrick, it follows the adventures of three young filmmakers, played by Michael C. Williams, Heather Donahue and Joshua Leonard. The trio head into the woods to try and uncover the mystery of local urban legend, the Blair Witch. They go missing, and only their equipment is found, together with the 'footage' they managed to shoot before their disappearance. The viewer then watches the recovered footage, and the story of what happened to the filmmakers is revealed. The film was groundbreaking in terms of its style. The recovered footage shown to the audience is filmed through the filmmakers' handheld camera, so the viewer feels as if they are watching a home movie. In the run up to the film's release the publicity was dealt with in such a way that the audience was not sure if the movie was a genuine filmmakers project, or Hollywood production. The producers started by leaking information about the project onto the internet, and allowing the hype to build from there. After the film's release the pretence was wearing thin, but the mythology of the Blair Witch had built up and audiences went in their droves to discover the fate of the young filmmakers. The film relied on the use of creepy props, natural sounds, the grainy quality of the footage and the 'real' performances of the actors (who were largely left to improvise the script, and deliberately deprived of food and sleep during filming) to strike fear into the audience. The Blair Witch is never seen, but her presence haunts the filmmakers throughout.

Sleepy Hollow
1999

Sleepy Hollow is directed by Tim Burton and based on 'The Legend of Sleepy Hollow', a short story written by Washington Irving in 1820, which was itself based upon an earlier German folk tale. Johnny Depp heads up this star-studded cast in the role of Ichabod Crane, a police constable who is summoned from New York to the upstate hamlet of Sleepy Hollow to investigate a series of brutal slayings. The perpetrator is widely rumoured to be a headless horseman, who returns to the site of his death each night to claim a mortal head in place of his missing one. In this film, and in the stories that inspired it, the horseman represents a real and present danger to the living inhabitants of Sleepy Hollow, and even after we have discovered that the real malice behind the plot comes from a living, breathing source, it is the ghoulish figure of the horseman that we most fear.

What Lies Beneath
2000

In *What Lies Beneath*, director Robert Zemeckis attempted to make a supernatural horror film that paid tribute to the work of Alfred Hitchcock in classics such as *Rear Window*, *Vertigo*, *Rebecca* and *Psycho*. The one major difference being that *What Lies Beneath* centred on a ghost story, an area Hitchock himself never explored. Michelle Pfeiffer, who is reminiscent of many of Hitchcock's clean-cut blonde actresses, plays Claire Spencer, the middle-aged wife of a renowned scientist and university professor, played by Harrison Ford. The couple move to Vermont following a serious car accident, the precise circumstances of which Claire cannot remember. Ghostly happenings begin to occur at their new house (doors opening and closing, pictures falling off walls, shadowy reflections) and Claire becomes convinced that either a ghost is trying to communicate with her, or she is losing her mind. Fearing for her sanity, she begins to investigate. Financially this film did very well, but critics remained unconvinced by its clichéd plotlines and were particularly critical of the gory end sequence, which some said was more laughable than scary. While this film may not live up to Hitchcock's masterpieces it does deliver some decent scares, even if they are mostly borrowed from other movies in the genre.

The Others
2001

This psychological horror was directed by Alejandro Amenabar and starred Nicole Kidman. Set in the period immediately after World War II, a woman waits in a remote country house for her husband to return from the war. New servants arrive at the house, they are furtive and the children, who suffer from an allergy to sunlight, appear at times to be possessed by spirits. The entire atmosphere of the film is one of gothic horror. Yet despite the traditional setting, the film plays on the ambiguity of the situation: is the woman going mad, are there really ghosts in the house, and, if so, who are they? *The Others* boasts a strong twist at the end, and although somewhat underrated, is thought by many critics to be a modern classic.

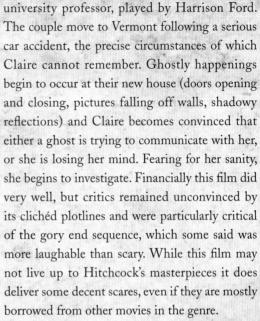

Watch your head! The legendary apparition of the Headless Horseman. *Sleepy Hollow* (1999).

The Grady girls from *The Shining* (1980). The actresses who played the girls, Lisa and Louise Burns, are identical twins; however, the characters in the book and film script are merely sisters, not twins.

Let the Children Play ! A woman brings her family back to her childhood home, where she opens an orphanage for handicapped children. Before long, her son Simon starts to communicate with invisible friends. Later she sees a mysterious masked boy and realizes that Simon has disappeared. *The Orphanage* (2007).

The Ring
2002

Another memorable film from this period, released in 2002, is *The Ring*, a remake of the 1998 Japanese horror movie *Ring*, which itself was based on the novel by Koji Suzuki. The film was directed by Gore Verbinski and stars Naomi Watts and Martin Henderson. Harking back to the time-honoured traditional ghost story, with the idea of a mysterious object that is cursed – in this case a videotape – the film is also up-to-date in style. The story concerns a journalist, Rachel Keller, who is recently divorced and is investigating a videotape that might hold a clue to the death of her niece and three of the girl's teenage friends. After watching the tape, she receives a phone call, and the voice of a young girl announces that she will die in seven days' time. Many twists and turns in the plot ensue, and Rachel eventually finds that her own life is threatened.

Before You Die, You See the Ring. An eerie promotional still from *The Ring* (2002).

The Haunted Mansion
2003

This American comedy horror movie was inspired by a ride of the same name located at Disney theme parks. It is aimed at a young audience so its scares are limited, but it features many elements synonymous with the ghost genre. The haunted mansion is situated in the bayou swamps of New Orleans, surrounded by fog and mist. The mansion is dark and creepy and contains secret passageways, a crystal ball with a gypsy trapped inside and spooky paintings on the walls. The classic twist is revealed when the family that are staying in the mansion learn that the residents are actually ghosts, bound to the property through a dreadful and tragic curse.

Just Like Heaven
2005

Reese Witherspoon and Mark Ruffalo star in this romantic fantasy directed by Mark Waters. The film opens with Elizabeth, a busy surgeon who is more interested in her career than her personal life. One night her sister, Abby, sets her up on a blind date which she reluctantly agrees to go on. On her way there she is involved in a car accident which leaves her in a coma and hooked up to a life support machine. A few months pass and David, a landscape architect, moves into her San Francisco apartment. David is grieving the death of his wife, and according to his best friend has stopped living. Soon after moving in, Elizabeth starts suddenly appearing and disappearing, and walking through walls. After conversations with David she eventually accepts that she is stuck somewhere between life and death. Together they begin to uncover what happened to her, and in the process start to fall in love. In one scene, David visits a book store to research Elizabeth's condition, when he meets Darryl, a spooky employee who seems to be able

to sense her presence. When David hears via the hospital that Abby plans to switch off Elizabeth's life support machine, David then realizes he must confront Abby with the truth. She does not believe him and he comes up with an elaborate plan to rescue the body before the machine is switched off. Miraculously, Elizabeth awakes from her coma, but sadly cannot remember David or any of their time together. David discovers that he was her blind date, and that he would have met her had she not been involved in that fateful car accident, and this leaves him heartbroken. Some time passes and David returns to the apartment having created a beautiful garden on the roof. Elizabeth finds him up there and at first is shocked, but when he passes her a key their hands touch and her memory is restored.

Throughout the film three characters can see or sense Elizabeth: David, Daryll and her niece. David is the only character who can see and talk to her. It is implied in several scenes that her youngest niece can sense her, in one memorable scene where the child is playing she asks Elizabeth if she would like some tea. Usually in ghost stories the spirit is bound to the home it lived in or the location it died in. Here, Elizabeth is free to go anywhere, and she can sit in a car without simply falling through it. Perhaps this is because Elizabeth is not technically a ghost in this film, she is somewhere between two worlds and as such is more of a spirit. This films deals with the idea of a type of 'limbo', somewhere a soul or spirit can wait until the body either recovers from a coma or dies. Here, Elizabeth's ghost is able to save her own life by communicating with the living, and in turn, remind David that life is for living.

Dark Water
2005

In 2005 an American remake of the Japanese movie *Dark Water* was made. It starred Jennifer Connelly, Pete Postlethwaite and Tim Roth, and

'What was once trapped, will now be unleashed.' Possessed by a Japanese onyro ghost, Kayako (Takako Fuji) returns from the grave to seek vengeance. *The Grudge 2* (2006).

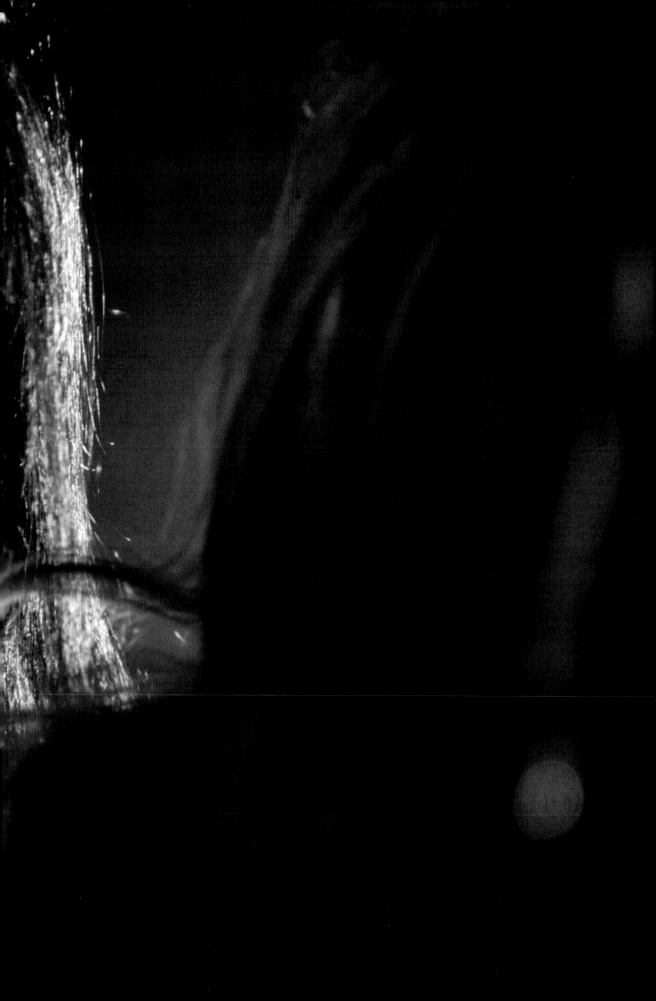

was directed by Walter Salles. The movie follows Dahlia (Connelly), who is in the middle of a bitter custody battle with her ex-husband Kyle over their daughter, Cecilia. Dahlia is desperate to keep the child, but Kyle claims Dahlia's debilitating migraines, and the fact that she was abused by her father and abandoned by her mother, mean that she is an unfit parent. Despite this, Dahlia and Cecilia move into a new apartment in a substandard building. On the roof sits a large water tank, and soon Dahlia's apartment starts to leak dark water. Investigating the apartment above her own, Dahlia discovers that a family named the Rimsky's lived there, and that their apartment was full of dark water. She finds a photo of the Rimsky's and notes that the little girl in the picture looks the same age as Cecilia. Soon after this, Dahlia starts having strange dreams in which Cecilia takes on the appearance of the Rimsky girl. Around the same time, Cecila begins to struggle at her new school because she is spending too much time talking to her imaginary friend, Natasha Rimsky. Dark water begins to flood Dahlia's apartment and at school Cecilia seems to be battling Natasha's influence while she paints her hand suddenly becomes controlled by an unseen force. Cecila goes to the bathroom which promptly floods with dark water and she passes out. Dahlia is unreachable and so Kyle is called to the scene and he takes Cecilia to his apartment. When Dahlia can't find her daughter she is frantic with worry, and her search leads her back onto the roof. She looks inside the water tank and discovers Natasha's body floating at the surface. The police arrive and conclude that Natasha died when she was abandoned by both parents, and, being unsupervised, came across the water tank which had been left open by the building's maintenance man. After this unpleasant episode, Dahlia decides to move out of the haunted building and move closer to Kyle. As

she is packing, Cecilia is having a bath. In the next scene, Dahlia is reading to the girl, who is wearing a hooded dressing gown. Suddenly, Dahlia hears Cecilia's voice from the bathroom, and realizes that the child she is sat with is Natasha. Dahlia runs to the bathroom, where Natasha pleads with Dahlia to be her mother forever, as she holds Cecilia down in the water. Dahlia agrees, on the condition that Natasha lets Cecilia live, Natasha lets her go and Dahlia drowns in the flooding apartment, fulfilling her promise. The ghosts of Dahlia and Natasha are then seen walking down the hallway. Later, Kyle and Cecilia return to the apartment to collect some of Cecilia's things. While they are in the elevator it briefly malfunctions and Cecilia has a flashback of her and her mother. Dahlia's ghost tells Cecilia she will always be with her, as she braids her hair. As Kyle and Cecilia get out of the elevator, he notices that her hair has been braided, and they quickly leave.

Paranormal Activity
2007

Paranormal Activity is an American supernatural horror film, and presented to the audience as 'found footage', using the same filming techniques utilized in *The Blair Witch Project*. The two main characters, Katie and Micah, set up a camera in their bedroom to capture the supernatural activity taking place in their house every night, and the audience sees what the camera has recorded. The ghostly presence, which conforms to the concept of a poltergeist, is sometimes referred to as a demon. It is invisible, has the ability to move objects and people, and makes odd, non-human footprints when treading through deliberately sprinkled talcum powder. Towards the end of the movie the idea of demonic possession is hinted on, perhaps a nod to *The Exorcist*. The movie was a box office success and a sequel has followed.

GHOSTS IN MUSIC

Ghosts are often mentioned in folk ballads, one famous example being 'The Unquiet Grave'. It tells the story of a lover mourning his true love on her grave for over a year, until the ghost of the young lady in question rouses herself and tells him to go away and leave her in peace. The moral of the story is that the dead should be mourned, remembered, and respected, but if grief continues for longer than 'a twelve month and a day' it disturbs the ghost of the loved one, and must be ended if he or she is to be left to rest in peace.

Another popular form of folk ballad is the 'night visiting song' that tells of ghosts coming back to see their loved ones, and then disappearing at dawn to go back to the land of the dead. One such ballad is 'The Grey Cock' which concerns a young woman. Asleep in her bed at night, she hears a knocking at her window and looks out to see her lover at the door. She comes down and lets him in to her room, where they spend the night together. However, she notices that his skin is unusually pale and his lips very cold. When she asks why, he tells her that he is the ghost of her lover, and that he must leave when the cock crows in the morning. She sends up a prayer, begging the cockerel not to crow, but her prayer is not answered, and the lover steals away, never to be seen again.

These ballads, and many others like them, were collected by Francis James Child in the late 19th century and published between 1882 and 1898 in ten volumes. They are mostly of English and Scottish origin, with American variants. Many of the folk songs concern supernatural events, as well as gruesome murders, noteworthy historical happenings, such as fierce battles, and stories about heroes such as Robin Hood and King Arthur.

Ghosts in Contemporary Music

Ghosts appear frequently in popular music, whether in rock and country classics or chart-oriented novelty songs. In some cases, as in the tale of the *Long Black Veil* or *(Ghost) Riders in the Sky*, they narrate ghost stories that draw from the folk ballads of the past, both in content and style; in others, they provide a metaphor for unrequited love, in time-honoured pop fashion.

(Ghost) Riders in the Sky: A Cowboy Legend
Vaughn Monroe, 1949

Country music is not short of songs about ghosts, and this is one of the most memorable. Written by the American songwriter and actor Stan Jones, it was recorded in 1949 by bandleader, trumpeter and singer Vaughn Monroe. Other versions, which number over 50, include releases by Bing Crosby, Johnny Cash, Peggy Lee, Spike Jones, Gene Autry and country rock band The Outlaws. The song tells of a herd of cattle stampeding in the sky, who are chased by the ghosts of cowboys long dead, in an image that resembles the ancient European folk tale of the Wild Hunt (see page 14).

Long Black Veil
Lefty Frizzell, 1959

This country ballad was written by songwriters Danny Dill and Marijohn Wilkin, and was first recorded by country star Lefty Frizzell. The tale is recounted in the voice of the ghost, in a style that harks back to traditional folk ballads. The story concerns a man who is falsely accused of murder, and who has an alibi – at the time of the murder, he was engaged in a secret tryst with his best friend's wife – but who refuses to reveal this fact, and thus is therefore executed. The ghost tells how the woman visits his grave in the dead of night, wearing a long black veil to hide her face. After its initial release, the song became a classic, and went on to be covered numerous times, perhaps most memorably by The Band and Johnny Cash.

Monster Mash
Bobby Pickett, 1962

This novelty song was released in 1962 and reached number one in the charts, coinciding with the Halloween celebrations for that year. Since then, it has continued to be a popular celebration of all things ghostly. The lyrics of the song mention ghouls, vampires and zombies, all of whom have been electrified into life by a mad scientist, and who go on to perform a bizarre, lumbering dance to the tune of the 'Monster Mash', which becomes 'a graveyard smash'.

There's a Ghost in My House
R. Dean Taylor, 1967

Canadian singer and songwriter R. Dean Taylor recorded this in 1967 with the Motown team Holland/Dozier/Holland. It didn't do as well as expected in the US, but in 1974 reached number three in the British charts. As with many pop songs, the phantom in question is the ghost of a lost love, who still haunts the melancholic singer.

Phantom 309
Red Sovine, 1967

Written by American singer and songwriter Tommy Faile and recorded in 1967 by Woodrow Wilson 'Red Sovine', a singer known for his truckdriving songs, the song narrates the tale of a poverty-stricken hitchhiker. He takes a ride with a man named 'Big Joe' who drives a tractor-trailer called 'Phantom 309'. After a long drive, the hitchhiker is dropped off at a truck stop, where he learns that Big Joe is the ghost of a man who swerved to avoid a bus full of children, costing him his life. A version of the song was later recorded by Tom Waits, among others.

Wuthering Heights
Kate Bush, 1978

In this song, Kate Bush imagines herself as the ghost of Cathy Earnshaw, a character in Emily Bronte's famous novel, *Wuthering Heights*.

Released as Kate Bush's first single, the song became a big hit, and catapulted her to success, appearing on her debut album *The Kick Inside*, released in 1978. Bush later explained that she had written the song aged just 18, after being inspired by watching the film version of the book; she also revealed that, at the time, she had been unsure of how to pronounce the word 'wuthering'.

Spirit in the Sky
Norman Greenbaum, 1979

This jaunty number was written and sung by Norman Greenbaum and released in 1979, going on to sell two million copies. In it, Greenbaum reflects on the afterlife, and on his certainty that when he dies, he will become a spirit, and go to live in heaven. It has been covered by many other bands since its original release, most notably perhaps by Doctor and the Medics.

Ghost Town
The Specials, 1981

In 1981, British ska band The Specials released this song, which became a number one hit. It is not literally a song about ghosts, but bemoans the decline of the band's home city of Coventry. Inner urban decay was a pressing issue in Britain at the time, as the manufacturing industries of many cities declined under the regime of the Conservative Prime Minister Margaret Thatcher. The song describes how the dance hall in the city has closed down, because of the frequent fighting that breaks out on the dance floor when bands come to play there. The spooky atmosphere and artwork of skeletons on the cover emphasized the ghostly imagery woven into the lyrics.

Ghostbusters
Ray Parker Junior, 1984

This was recorded in 1984 as the accompanying theme tune to the *Ghostbusters* film, and was a massive hit, staying at number one in the US charts for three weeks. Ray Parker Junior was later sued by Huey Lewis, of Huey Lewis and the News, who claimed that it was derived from a guitar riff on a song of his called 'I Want a New Drug'. The dispute was eventually settled out of court.

The Ghost of Tom Joad
Bruce Springsteen, 1995

The title track of Bruce Springsteen's album of the same name, this was inspired by John Steinbeck's *The Grapes of Wrath* and by Woody Guthrie's *Ballad of Tom Joad*. The subject of the song, which is performed here in an eerie, acoustic setting, is the legacy of poverty and unemployment inherited from the Depression years in America. In 1998, the song was released as a single by Rage Against the Machine, who gave it a more raucous, aggressive treatment.

Other ghost-inspired songs

Ghosts, Laura Marling
Ghosts, Randy Newman
Haunted, The Pogues and Sinead O'Connor
Is There a Ghost, Band of Horses
Little Ghost, White Stripes
Same Ghost Every Night, Wolf Parade
Supernatural, Madonna
Walking With a Ghost, Tegan and Sara

Demons terrorize Jan and Mark Montelli (Erica and Brent Katz) in *Amityville II: The Possession* (1982)

INDEX

IMAGE CREDITS

ISBN: 978-1-907795-06-0

Canary Press
An imprint of Omnipress Ltd
Chantry House, 22 Upperton Road
Eastbourne, East Sussex BN21 1BF
England

Printed and bound in China.

10 9 8 7 6 5 4 3 2 1

Indexer: Hazel Young
Production manager: Benita Estevez
Editor: Jennifer Davies
Cover and internal design: Anthony Prudente